PRAISE FOR THE
UNCOMMON JUNIOR HIGH GROUP STUDIES

M000101919

The best junior high/middle school curriculum to come out in years.
Jim Burns, Ph.D.
President, HomeWord

A landmark resource for years to come.
Chapman R. Clark, Ph.D.
Associate Professor of Youth and Family Ministry
Fuller Theological Seminary

The *Uncommon* Junior High curriculum is truly "cross-cultural." Built on the solid foundation of an understanding of junior-highers' unique developmental needs and rapidly changing culture, it affords teachers and youth workers the opportunity to communicate God's unchanging Word to kids growing up in a world that increasingly muffles and muddles the truth.
Walt Mueller
President, Center for Parent/Youth Understanding
Author of *Understanding Today's Youth Culture*

The creators and writers of this curriculum know and love young teens, and that's what sets good junior high curriculum apart from the mediocre stuff!
Mark Oestreicher
President, Youth Specialties

This is serious curriculum for junior-highers! Not only does it take the great themes of the Christian faith seriously, but it takes junior-highers seriously as well.
Wayne Rice
Founder and Director, Understanding Your Teenager Seminars

It fleshes out . . . two absolute essentials for great curriculum: biblical depth and active learning.
Duffy Robbins
Associate Professor, Department of Youth Ministry
Eastern College

THE
LIFE OF
JESUS

uncommon
be extraordinary.

THE
LIFE OF
JESUS

KARA POWELL
General Editor

Published by Gospel Light
Ventura, California, U.S.A.
www.gospellight.com
Printed in the U.S.A.

Previously published as Pulse #4: *Teachings of Jesus* and
Pulse #8: *Miracles of Jesus.*

Contributing writers: Kara Powell, Ph.D.; Natalie Chenault;
Miles McPherson; Amberly Neese, Siv Ricketts.

Library of Congress Cataloging-in-Publication Data
Powell, Kara Eckmann, 1970-
Uncommon junior high group study : the life of Jesus / Kara Powell, general editor.
p. cm.
ISBN 978-0-8307-4643-9 (trade paper)
1. Jesus Christ—Biography—Study and teaching. 2. Church group work with teenagers.
3. Christian education of teenagers. 4. Church group work with preteens.
5. Christian education of preteens. I. Title.
BT307.P712 2009
268'.433—dc22
2008047316

Rights for publishing this book outside the U.S.A. or in non-English languages are
administered by Gospel Light Worldwide, an international not-for-profit ministry.
For additional information, please visit www.glww.org, email info@glww.org, or write
to Gospel Light Worldwide, 1957 Eastman Avenue, Ventura, CA 93003, U.S.A.

Contents

How to Use the *Uncommon* Junior High Group Studies

Each *Uncommon* junior high group study contains 12 sessions, which are divided into 2 stand-alone units of 6 sessions each. You may choose to teach all 12 sessions consecutively, or to use just one unit, or to present each session separately. You know your group, so do what works best for you and your students.

This is your leader's guidebook for teaching your group. Electronic files (in PDF format) of each session's student handouts are available on the junior high edition of *The Life of Jesus* DVD. The handouts include the "Reflect" section of each study, formatted for easy printing, in addition to any student worksheets for the session. You may print as many copies as you need for your group.

Each individual session begins with a brief overview of the "big idea" of the lesson, the aims of the session, the primary Bible verse and additional verses that tie in to the topic being discussed. Each of the 12 sessions is geared to be 45 to 90 minutes in length and is comprised of two options that you can choose from, based on the type of group that you have. Option 1 tends to be a more active learning experience, while Option 2 tends to be a more discussion-oriented exercise.

The sections in each session are as follows:

Starter

Young people will stay in your youth group longer if they feel comfortable and make friends. This first section helps students get to know each other better and focus on the theme of the lesson in a fun and engaging way. After the Starter, you can show the introduction to the session from Kara Powell on *The Life of Jesus* DVD.

Message

The Message section enables students to look up to God by relating the words of Scripture to the session topic.

Dig

Unfortunately, many young people are biblically illiterate. In this section, students look inward and discover how God's Word connects with their own world.

Apply

Young people need the opportunity to think through the issues at hand. The apply section leads students out into their world with specific challenges to apply at school, at home and with their friends.

Reflect

This concluding section of the study allows students to reflect on the material presented in the session. You can print these pages from the PDF found on *The Life of Jesus* DVD and give them to your students as a handout for them to work on during the week.

Want More Options?
An additional option for each section, along with accompanying worksheets, is available in PDF format on *The Life of Jesus* DVD.

UNIT I

The Miracles of Jesus

Your God Is Too Small. The title of J. B. Phillips's book continues to haunt me. *Your God Is Too Small*. I have never even read the book, and I have no idea what lies beyond its cover, but I think of its title often. Is my God too small? Have I boxed Him in? Squeezed Him into categories I'm comfortable with and can understand? Made Him unoriginal, mundane and *ordinary*?

What about the God that your students know? Is He too small? Whether they've grown up in the church or are new to the faith, have they caught that contagious chill of tradition, routine and predictability? I pray this study will help them shake it off. Or rather that the Book talked about in this study will cure them of the spiritual blahs that can creep up and leave them dull and listless. Or—even more accurately—that the Author of the Book will do that.

The aim of this study is to expose students to the divine Author and His Son, Jesus, in their perfect balance between nearness and farness. By "nearness" I mean the too-good-to-be-true fact that God wanted relationships with us so badly that He sent Jesus to live with us, giving us the opportunity to draw near to Him. But it's not just His nearness that makes Him God. It's His farness. Some students have lost sight of the truth that Jesus is not a teddy bear who exists to make us feel better about ourselves. He is wholly other—*the* Holy Other—who demonstrates His power in ways that should make us shake in our shoes.

It's a good thing that in Jesus' miracles, He demonstrated His Father's nearness and farness by using that holy might to relieve and help those He cared about, including the paralyzed, the blind and the crippled. He still helps us today—from the eighth grader who hears her parents fighting every night as she lies in bed and is just sure they're on the verge of divorce, to the seventh grader who prays every day for his best friend who is Mormon. Then there's the youth worker who has had a long day and wants more than anything else to simply go home and rest, but instead loves, serves and teaches junior-highers about the miracles of Jesus.

Although we've packed this study full of teaching tips, strategies, discussions, object lessons, games, illustrations and activities to help your students understand Jesus' miracles, I'd like to give you a few more tips to help students walk out of your meetings and be able to say:

- *This one's not computer-generated.* Computer graphic capabilities have blurred fact and fiction by making the impossible *seem* possible. Yet computers only make videos, movies and actors *seem* transformed. Jesus *does* transform, bringing new eyes, new legs and new relationships. In order to help your students understand that these miracles are *real*, take advantage of our suggestions to have them feel the mud on their hands, let the water run through their fingers and imagine what it's like to be without sight. The more tangible you can make your teaching, the more you can engage their senses, the more you help them feel as if they were actually there—the more they'll remember. Maybe more importantly, the more they'll *believe*.

- *This one's happened to me.* We know junior-highers, but we don't know *your* junior-highers. Some of them have had miracles happen to them or to people they know. It might be a physical healing, a relational reconciliation or an emotional breakthrough. Invite your students to share *real life* stories of ways they've seen the enormity of God.

- *This one means something to me.* Please do not cut response time short. Don't try to squeeze it in at the end of the meeting, as students start looking at their watches and rides begin to show up. Let students figure out what the miracle you're talking about means to them, how it shakes their world and what it does to their view of God.

May our God and all of our students' God be *huge*.

Kara Powell
Director of the Center for Youth and Family Ministry
Assistant Professor of Youth, Family and Culture
Fuller Theological Seminary

DEAD MAN WALKING

THE BIG IDEA

Jesus cares deeply about what you're going through and wants to help.

SESSION AIMS

In this session you will guide students to (1) understand the depth of God's desire to help in times of trouble; (2) feel a peace from knowing that the plans of God supercede their finite plans; and (3) act by acknowledging that Christ is in control of one specific, difficult area of their lives.

THE BIGGEST VERSE

"When Jesus saw her weeping, and the Jews who had come along with her also weeping, He was deeply moved in spirit and troubled" (John 11:33).

OTHER IMPORTANT VERSES

Luke 10:38-42; John 1:28; 4:43-54; 8:58; 10:40; 11:1-57; 12:9-11; Hebrews 4:15; James 1:2-4

STARTER

Option 1: Infiltration. You need a large outdoor area to play the game (the larger, the better), four adult volunteers, a stopwatch, 3x5-inch index cards, candy for prizes, one pen in each of the following colors: black, red, blue, green and orange, and one piece of sidewalk chalk in each of the following colors: white, red, blue, green and orange.

Ahead of time, use the white chalk to divide a large, rectangular area into four sectors equal in size and large enough to accommodate a group of students; then use the other colors to draw a "+" (plus sign) in the sectors, designating each sector's (and each group's) color.

At the meeting, greet students and divide them into four groups. Assign an adult to each group. Distribute the index cards to students and a colored pen to each of the four adults (you keep the black pen). Have each group stand in the sector corresponding to the colored pen that the group's leader has. One sector will be the Green Sector, one the Red Sector, and so on.

Explain that the object of the game is to reach all opposing teams' leaders (adults) without being tagged (a two-hand touch) by a member of another team. Once a leader has been successfully reached, he or she marks a "+" (plus sign) on the infiltrator's card. Each opposing team's plus sign is worth five points. When players have their cards marked by all three opposing teams, they can return to their own sectors without being tagged.

If a player is tagged while trying to enter an opposing team's sector, he or she must be taken to home base (the middle of the playing field), where you mark his or her card with a black "-" (minus sign). Each minus sign is worth *negative* two points. He or she must then start again in his or her team's sector.

At the end of the game, the team with the least amount of points scored against it wins 20 points, plus whatever points its members accumulated.

Signal the beginning of the game; then allow 12 minutes of play. Add up the scores and award the prizes to the winning team. Then discuss the following questions:

- Which strategies worked most effectively?
- Which ones didn't work at all?

Point out that although we don't always understand the methods or strategies of others, it's not necessary for us to understand something for it to be effective. The same is true with the methods God uses in our lives: Although we don't always understand or agree with them, we should be willing to learn from

His methods and know that God desires to be a "home base" for all of us in our times of difficulty.

Option 2: Which Switch Is Which? You need copies of "Which Switch Is Which?" found on the next page (this is also available as a PDF on *The Life of Jesus* DVD) and some students who are up to the challenge of abstract thinking!

Distribute "Which Switch Is Which?" and then divide students into groups of two or three. Inform the groups that they have four minutes to come up with some possible solutions to the problem on the handout.

After four minutes, ask for volunteers to discuss solutions that they came up with. (*Note*: Avoid potential embarrassment for those who just didn't get it by inviting only those students who are obviously willing to share their solutions.) If no one has come up with the correct solution, discuss the following solution with the group. Here's the solution:

> *First, flip one of the three switches to the On position and leave it on for 10 to 15 minutes; then flip it to the off position. Next, flip one of the other two switches to the On position and open the door to the room. Of course, the light that's on corresponds to the switch that you just flipped on! Here's where the original switch you flipped comes in: One of the two lights that is now off will have a warm bulb; that light is controlled by the original switch. The cool bulb belongs to the light controlled by the switch you never touched! Simple, huh? (Yeah, right!)*

After you've revealed the solution, explain that sometimes we try to figure out how situations could or should be resolved. We don't always see all the possibilities, but God does. Like we're going to see today, His planning is perfect, and He knows the solution before we even have a problem.

MESSAGE

Option 1: The Right Tools for the Job. For this option, you will need several Bibles, three adult volunteers, three random props (for instance, a feather duster, a plunger and an oddly shaped pillow) and a bunch of students who really like to ham it up.

Ask the three adult volunteers to come forward; then select six student volunteers (ideally, three guys and three girls). Divide the volunteers into three teams: guys, girls and adults. Have the adults' team, the girls' team and one

Which Switch
Is Which?

You are in a room with three switches and a door. The switches are across the room from the door and you cannot touch the switches and hold the door open simultaneously. These switches correspond to three lights in an adjoining room (on the other side of the door). You want to figure out which switch goes with which light. It can be done by only opening the door one time. How is this possible?

Solution: First, flip one of the three switches to the On position and leave it on for 10 to 15 minutes; then flip it to the Off position. Next, flip one of the other two switches to the On position and open the door to the room. Of course, the light that's on corresponds to the switch you just flipped on! Here's where the original switch comes in: One of the two lights that is now off will have a warm bulb; that light is controlled by the original switch. The cool bulb belongs to the light controlled by the switch you never touched!

student from the guys' team leave the room, and then explain to the two remaining volunteers (and the rest of the students) that the "audience" is going to call out two things: a need that people have (such as a drink of water or food) and a random place (such as a sinking ship or a football field). The two volunteers are to act out (no talking allowed) the suggested *need* at the suggested *place* and continue acting while you bring the other male volunteer back into the room.

Call the guys' teammate back into the room and hand him one of the props. Instruct him to use the prop and join in the action with his teammates. Remind all three students that there is absolutely *no talking*! Allow a couple of minutes of pantomime; then stop the action and ask the student what he thought he was doing and where it was taking place.

Invite two of the members from the girls' team back into the room and repeat the process with the girls' team, and then do the same with the adults. Congratulate the team that did the best job getting that third clueless teammate to join in and guess the right need and place.

Invite everyone to regroup. Distribute the Bibles as you point out that it's tough to have a need and not have the right tools to fit that need. Ask for a few volunteers to read John 11:1-44 aloud, and then suggest that Jesus probably visited Mary and Martha's house regularly (see v. 11). Lazarus's sickness must have been pretty severe for them to send for Jesus and ask Him to come back to Bethany, even though the people there were ready to kill Him (see v. 8).[1] Discuss the following:

1. Why would Jesus be glad that He was not present when Lazarus had died (see vv. 14-15)? *He knew this would be an opportunity for a demonstration of His power; He knew God would use it to build up the faith of His disciples, Mary and Martha and others.*

2. Jesus' reputation as a healer was obviously well known (see v. 37), so some of the crowd was frustrated that He hadn't come earlier.

Youth Leader Tip

A great way to make visitors feel welcome is to provide name tags when students arrive. Allow everyone to pick a superhero, cartoon character, celebrity or professional athlete. They will have to work hard at remembering each others' names, and visitors will feel less different.

What do Martha's words in John 11:21-27 and 39 reveal about her faith? *Although she had a relationship with Jesus, she lacked faith in who He was. In her mind she thought Jesus really couldn't do much to change the fact that her brother had been dead for four days. She understood that there would be a resurrection of the dead at the end of the world (see vv. 21-27), but did not believe Jesus could raise her brother after four days.*

3. What does Jesus' prayer in verses 41 and 42 say about His faith? *He knew that He could count on His Father to come through for Him.*

Transition to the next step by explaining that next you're going to see how Jesus' words and actions can impact us 2,000 years later.

Option 2: In God's Time. For this option, you will need several Bibles.

Select two or three volunteers. One at a time, have each of them stand in a doorway with their hands to their sides (palms against their legs). While standing in the doorway, each volunteer is to press the tops of his or her hands against the doorframe as hard as possible for one minute. When you signal that the minute is over, he or she will step away from the doorway and relax—his or her arms will float upward unaided (due to the blood rushing back into the arms). Explain that often when we stop trying so hard and let go, God can do amazing things.

Distribute the Bibles and read John 11:1-44 together, and then ask students to sit in a large circle. Instruct them to retell the story of the raising of Lazarus one word at a time (i.e., the first person might say "Lazarus." The next person could say "died.") Continue around the circle until the story is finished.

Took a long time, right? Point out that by the time Jesus got there, Lazarus had been dead for four days. The normal procession of family, friends and mourners had already been grieving for those four days. Martha went to meet Jesus, as might be expected, while Mary went to Jesus when Martha told her that He was asking for her (see Luke 10:38-42 for another example of the sisters' typical reactions).

Next, discuss the following questions with the group:

1. What might the disciples have been feeling about Jesus' actions? *They were probably confused or puzzled about why Jesus, their friend, did not immediately leave for Mary and Martha's, or they might have*

wondered why He didn't just heal Lazarus from a distance, as He had done for others. They also knew His life was in danger.

2. What do you think the sisters might have been thinking about Jesus? *They also knew Jesus could have stopped the death of their brother, even from 20 miles away! They were probably confused and hurt that He had not healed Lazarus, as He had done for so many others, even from a distance.*

3. What does Martha's reaction to Jesus' command to "take away the stone" tell you about her faith? *Martha still did not have a complete understanding of Jesus' power over life and death. She was still being the practical, realistic one, knowing that the reality was that her brother had been dead four days.*

4. What would you be thinking if you had witnessed this event and the miracle? *(Remind students that they have the advantage of hearing this story after the ending is known. Try to get them to place themselves realistically in the situation.)*

5. What does the fact that Lazarus walked out of the tomb after being dead four days do to your own faith? *(Allow some discussion on this. You will probably get a wide variety of reactions from complete acceptance of this miracle to complete skepticism.)*

Explain that Jesus could have healed Lazarus right away and stopped the suffering his death caused, but instead, Jesus chose to wait. Sometimes we are allowed to go through a certain amount of hardship so that when God reveals His glory, we can see His power in our lives. Jesus knew that the four days He waited to go to Lazarus's tomb would be an extremely hard time for Lazarus's family, but He also knew that the awesome power of the Father would be obvious when He raised Lazarus from the dead, demonstrating that He was "the resurrection and the life."

Conclude the discussion by suggesting that God sometimes allows difficult things to happen to us in our lives in order to strengthen us and to build our faith. In sports, athletes use resistance to build muscles, and the same is true with our spiritual lives. Our spiritual muscles are strengthened through resistance and difficulty.

DIG

Option 1: Big and Small. For this option, read the following case study aloud to your group:

Allison was always mature for her age. She developed early, was smarter and looked years older than the majority of the others at her junior high. Other girls were very threatened by Allison. They would gossip about her behind her back, claiming that she lacked morals or that she had flunked a few grades. Deep inside, however, they all knew that they were jealous of her.

Allison got the attention of the boys as well. The guys would joke with each other about which one of them would ask her out, but ultimately no one did. In fact, there were many days that went by when no one—male or female—would talk to her at all.

Chris had the opposite problem, but suffered the same torment from his classmates. He was the junior-high student that didn't grow much after third grade. Even though his doctor said he would grow again soon, he was faced every day with rude jokes and comments about being short. He was miserable.

Now discuss the following:

1. What do Allison and Chris have in common? *Actually, they have the same problem that all teens have: They can't control the internal clocks that their bodies run by! Allison's maturation schedule is rapid, while Chris's is lethargic and slow. Neither of them has any control over how fast they are growing and maturing, but both are ridiculed by their peers because of it.*

2. What do you think Jesus would feel about what they're going through? *Jesus walked on earth as a man and experienced every emo-*

Youth Leader Tip

When using scenarios like the one above, select students from the audience as models. You can even have students dress in costumes or provide other props for them to act out the story and explain the story in a visual way to the group. This helps to grab their attention.

tion we do (see Hebrews 4:15). He empathizes with us, feeling emotions as we do. Although He could see the eventual outcome of their situations, He would understand and feel their suffering.

3. What might He say to them? *Get over it! No, seriously—He'd probably tell them to have faith that, as difficult as it might be, they are both maturing at a rate determined by God for reasons only He understands—and that they are loved by Him exactly as they are, regardless of how others see them.*

Option 2: Details of a Miracle. For this option, ask your students the following questions:

1. What reasons might Jesus have had for not raising Lazarus on the first day? *There are lots of them: It was important that there was no doubt that Lazarus was truly dead. Jesus was also aware that His crucifixion wasn't far off, so it's possible that He was demonstrating God's power over death. Finally, everyone involved learned more about faith through the experience and many actually came to faith because of Lazarus's death and resurrection (see John 11:42,45).*

2. Why does God allow bad things to happen to us? *There are certain things that happen for a purpose we may never understand. We do have God's assurance, though, that He is making us stronger in our faith through those experiences. As James 1:2-4 teaches, "Consider it pure joy, my brothers, when you face trials of many kinds, because you know that the testing of your faith develops perseverance. Perseverance must finish its work so that you may be mature and complete, not lacking anything."*

3. What reasons might Jesus have for crying over Lazarus's death, as described in John 11:35, if He knew that He was going to bring him back to life? *He must have felt the sadness of those around; after all, He was good friends with Lazarus and his sisters and probably felt empathy for those who were mourning. He might have also been saddened that people still didn't believe in Him and His power to perform miracles. He may have been angry over the realities of sin and death caused by His enemy, Satan.*

4. In verse 42, Jesus said, "I knew that you always hear me, but I said this for the benefit of the people standing here." Does that mean it's okay to pray just so others can see you and hear you? *You should never pray just for show; however, praying aloud in earnest thanksgiving and praise to God can be an awesome teaching tool for unbelievers to understand the power and purpose of prayer and to recognize His answers. His prayer made people take notice and consider the source of His heavenly power—our heavenly Father.*

APPLY

Option 1: Putting Lazarus in the Tomb. For this option, you will need a miniature coffin made out of a shoebox that has been cut and pasted into the shape of a coffin (and then painted to resemble one). You will also need colored paper and pens or pencils. (If there's no time to make the coffin beforehand, just use the shoebox as is.)

Distribute colored paper and pens or pencils as you point out that Jesus proved that He had the power to raise Lazarus from the dead (see John 11). If He is powerful enough to do that, He can certainly help students in the areas of their lives that are difficult.

Turn their attention to the coffin and explain that just like Lazarus in his tomb, our struggles in life are not out of Jesus' reach or ability to help. Ask students to write down one area of their life that they want God's help in—maybe it's a relationship that's gone bad; perhaps they're struggling with their parents about certain areas of their life; maybe there are things at school that are hard to handle. Whatever it is, God cares and wants to help. Allow a couple of minutes for students to write their problems; then invite them to come forward and place their papers in the coffin.

After everyone has come forward, remind students that Jesus waited four days before raising Lazarus—days that must have seemed endless for the mourners—so their situations may not be remedied overnight. They can be sure, though, that God will work in that area.

Option 2: Prayer Reminder. You need pieces of black construction paper and several pens with white, gold or silver ink (these can be found at most office or craft supply stores). *Economy Option:* White, yellow, gold or silver crayons or pencils may be more affordable—anything that will show up on the black paper is okay.

Explain that sometimes we feel as if we're the only ones in the world who have to deal with tough situations, but the truth is that people all around us have struggles, too. Tough situations can look pretty dark for those who don't have the comfort that knowing Jesus gives.

Distribute the construction paper and pens and explain that the black paper symbolizes the pain and problems of people who don't know Jesus yet. Instruct students to think about someone they know who's going through a tough time right now and doesn't know Jesus. Invite them to draw a picture on their paper that symbolizes the person they have in mind (this might include their initials, but not their full name).

Remind students that just as they can see what they have drawn on the black paper, the Good News of Jesus stands out in dark times. Ask students to place their papers where they will see them and be reminded to pray for others who are going through tough times.

Close in prayer, asking God that all of the people symbolized on the papers would be led to Jesus' comfort and help.

REFLECT

The following short devotions are for the students to reflect on and answer during the week. You can make a copy of these pages and distribute to your class or print out from the PDF for this session found on *The Life of Jesus* DVD.

1—TURN TO HIM

Need help? Discover who has some for you in Psalm 46:1-3.

Kelly felt as if her life was falling apart. The factory where her mom and dad worked closed down and both her parents lost their jobs. Her family had to move into a smaller house in order to save money, and they scrimped on everything. Kelly's parents were unable to find work. The stress of the situation began to take its toll and it seemed they fought constantly.

After a few months, Kelly's parents decided to get a divorce. Her mother was moving to California, her father was moving to Connecticut and it was up to Kelly to decide which parent she wanted to live with. She felt so alone and confused, because no one she knew seemed to understand what she was going through.

God cares about all our suffering. He wants desperately for us to turn to Him when we're in need and tell Him what's going on.

Do you turn to Him when you're in trouble and tell Him everything that's happening? Why or why not?

_____

_____

_____

_____

_____

_____

What is one thing that you can share with Him right now?

_____

_____

_____

_____

_____

2—WHERE DO YOU HIDE?

Who will keep you strong? Look up 1 Corinthians 1:8-9 to find out.

Imagine that you're caught in a terrible storm. Wind is stinging your face, rain is pelting your body and you're freezing cold. Where would you hide?

- ❑ Under a piece of newspaper
- ❑ In a shack with no door and broken windows
- ❑ Inside the local 24-hour grocery store
- ❑ Under a scrawny, leafless tree

Sometimes life can feel like a terrible storm—and we're trapped smack-dab in the middle. God says that He is our place to hide in times of trouble, but we can easily get distracted and hide in other places: watching TV, sleeping, playing video games, school—even friends and family.

Where do you hide from life's turmoil?

_____

_____

_____

_____

_____

Pray that God will remind you to hide in Him as you walk through the storms of life.

3—GOD REMEMBERS

Look up 1 Thessalonians 5:23-24 and find out who called you.

Andrew's mom was one thoughtful gal. She remembered to pick him up from school—even on half days and when he had to stay late for band practice. She remembered that he hated tuna and never packed it in his lunch. She even remembered that he asked her not to call him Andy-bear-baby in front of his friends. Andy was extremely glad that his mom remembered everything that was important to him because that made him feel that he was important to her.

God remembers all the promises He made to us and He is faithful to His Word. It can be hard to see that when times are hard—when we are sick, when everything is going wrong or when someone we love has died—but God has promised to be there for us always, especially when we're hurting.

Thank God for always being there for you and pray that you will remember to turn to Him when you are in need.

4—GOD COMFORTS US

Find 2 Corinthians 1:3-4 as fast as you can!

Imagine that your best friend has a nasty cold and you're planning a visit to cheer him or her up. What will you bring to comfort your friend? (Check all that apply.)

- ❏   His or her favorite magazine
- ❏   A giant bottle of hot sauce
- ❏   Your dirty laundry
- ❏   Cough drops
- ❏   Tissues
- ❏   His or her least favorite candy bar

God comforts us in our times of trouble. He also uses us to comfort others.

Do you know anyone who's going through a tough time? Maybe you have a friend or a neighbor who could use some comforting. What's one way you can comfort them today and show God's love?

_____

_____

_____

_____

_____

THE MAIN THING

THE BIG IDEA

Jesus values helping people more than following the expectations, traditions and religious rules of others.

SESSION AIMS

In this session you will guide students to (1) understand the priorities of Christ; (2) be motivated to prioritize human needs over others' expectations, traditions and religious rules; and (3) act by identifying one way they can obey Christ's most important rules of loving God and loving others.

THE BIGGEST VERSE

"Then Jesus said to them, 'I ask you, which is lawful on the Sabbath: to do good or to do evil, to save life or to destroy it?' He looked around at them all, and then said to the man, 'Stretch out your hand.' He did so, and his hand was completely restored. But they were furious and began to discuss with one another what they might do to Jesus" (Luke 6:9-11).

OTHER IMPORTANT VERSES

Genesis 2:2, 3; Exodus 20:8-11; 31:12-17; 34:21; Deuteronomy 23:25; 1 Samuel 21:1-6; Matthew 5:17,18; 16:24-26; 22:34-40; Mark 3:6; Luke 6:1-11; John 15:10,18-21; 2 Timothy 3:12; Hebrews 4:15; 5:8

STARTER

Option 1: Rule Breakers. You need a chair for each student. Set up the chairs in several rows ahead of time.

At the meeting, greet students and invite them to be seated, and then ask for a show of hands as you ask: How many of you like rules? (Be very suspicious of anyone who raises his or her hand!) Continue by asking how many in the group sometimes break rules. Let students know that you're going to do an exercise that will help them to think about the types of rules they tend to break. You're going to read some statements and students need to move as directed by what you read.

For every rule that students *have* broken, they must move seats as you instruct (e.g., "one seat to the left"). If they *have not* broken the rule, they stay in the same spot. If someone is already sitting in the seat where they are trying to move, both must share the seat. (It will get tight as more students pile up!) If students are sitting on the end of a row and are told to move in that direction, they must move to the other end. If they reach the front or the back during play, they must run to the opposite end. Read the following directions:

- If you've ever jaywalked by crossing a street where there wasn't a crosswalk, move one seat to your right.

- If you've ever eaten in a place where you weren't supposed to, move three seats back.

- If you've ever watched a TV show or movie you weren't supposed to watch, move two seats to your left.

- If you've ever copied someone's homework instead of doing your own, move four seats to your right.

- If you've ever asked for a bathroom pass at school when all you really wanted was an excuse to leave class, move two seats behind you and one seat to your right.

- If you've ever crossed the street even though the sign said "Don't Walk," move three seats behind you.

- If you've ever left your house without your parents' knowing, move two seats to your right and three seats in front of you.

- If you've ever tried to hide a report card, test or paper from your parents, move two seats to your left and five seats back.

- If you've ever borrowed your brother's or sister's stuff when you weren't supposed to, move three seats forward and two seats to your left.

Have students return to their original seats; then discuss:

1. If you had the chance to design a few rules that everybody in the world would have to live by, what would they be?

2. What do you think makes a good rule? *A good answer here would be something that protects or helps people.*

3. Is it ever okay to break rules? Explain.

As you transition to the next step, let the students know that today you're going to see that our best role model, Jesus, at times broke a few cultural rules. But He always did it for the right reason, and before they leave, they'll understand exactly what that right reason is.

Option 2: Rule Charades. You need a whiteboard, a dry-erase marker, five small pieces of paper for each student, pens or pencils, a container to hold the papers and a stopwatch.

Greet students and give them each five small pieces of paper and a pen or pencil. Divide the group into two equal teams and ask each team to select five representatives.

Instruct students to write the name of a famous person or fictional character on each piece of paper they have. It has to be someone who is pretty well known. Remind them that their writing needs to be legible and they shouldn't share the names they write down with anyone else. When they are done, tell them to fold the papers in half and place them in the container.

After everyone is done and all papers are collected and placed in the container, have the five representatives from each team line up and explain that the first person in each line will play Round One, the second will play Round Two, and so forth, until all five team representatives have played.

Explain that in Round One, there are no rules except that the player may not at any time say the person's name. He or she can give whatever clues they like, including impersonations, words that the names sound like and biographical information. Each team's first representative will have one minute to describe as many people as he or she can to the rest of his or her team. Only that team is eligible to guess. When a person's name is correctly guessed, the representative moves on to the next name. At the end of the minute, the number of names correctly identified equals the number of points the team receives. If the team is in the middle of guessing a name when the time elapses, that name doesn't count.

After Round One is completed, explain that in Round Two, all team representatives must *sing* their clues. Absolutely no talking allowed, just singing. It doesn't have to rhyme or sound good. Same rules for time and guessing apply.

After Round Two is over, explain that in Round Three, team representatives *cannot use any body language* to convey ideas. Doing so results in the loss of two points per offense. Same rules for time and guessing apply.

After Round Three is done, explain that in Round Four, team representatives can *only* use body language to convey ideas—no words or sounds. Same rules for time and guessing apply.

After Round Four is completed, explain that in Round Five, only one-syllable words may be used. The use of a two-or-more-syllable word means the team representative has to stop speaking and move on to the next name.

Add up the five scores from each team and determine a winner, and then discuss the following:

1. What purpose did the rules serve in this game?

2. How do you feel about rules in general?

3. What purpose do rules serve? *A good answer here is that rules protect people.*

Explain that God made some rules, but these laws were not designed to make Christianity boring or difficult. Instead, they were designed to protect our relationship with Him. Sometimes people in the Bible got the purpose of rules mixed up, so Jesus had to straighten them out.

MESSAGE

Option 1: Balancing Act. You need some well-balanced students.

Explain that God made some rules for people in the Old Testament to protect their relationships with Him, to keep them wholly devoted to Him and to keep them pure. Let's pretend that God gave us this rule: *In order to grow in your relationship with Me, you have to stand on one leg. As long as you are standing on only one leg, you can have a close relationship with Me.* Demonstrate by standing like a stork on one leg and continue:

Ask all of the students to participate. Have fun with this, seeing who can stand on one leg the longest. As you continue the balancing act, ask students what is on their minds the most: their relationship with God or how to keep standing on one leg?

When everyone has been eliminated (or when you're ready to move on), explain that while obviously God didn't give a rule in the Old Testament that you had to stand on one leg, some of the Jews in Bible times started focusing on the rules instead of their relationship with God.

People mixed man-made rules with God's laws, causing them to be so focused on obeying the rules that they forgot the purpose of the rules to begin with, which was to protect their relationships with God and to help them grow closer to Him.

Ask for a volunteer to read Luke 6:1-11 aloud, and then share the following background and contextual information about the rules:

In Luke 5, Jesus angered the Pharisees by claiming to forgive the paralytic's sins, something they understood only God could do. As a result, the Pharisees began to follow Jesus around, watching Him like hawks to see if He would break any more rules, especially the man-made rules about doing work on the Sabbath.

The rule against work on the Sabbath was very important to the Jews: It had roots in the creation account (Genesis 2:2; 3); it was specifically mentioned in the Ten Commandments (Exodus 20:8-11); and it was specifically defined in hundreds of man-made interpretations and traditions.[1] They figured it would be easy to catch Jesus breaking Sabbath rules. They wouldn't have to wait long.

In Luke 6:1-2, we read that the Pharisees accused the disciples of breaking the Sabbath by threshing grain they had picked. Picking grain from a field for a snack was okay (see Deuteronomy 23:25), but according to their interpretation of Exodus 34:21, rubbing the heads of

Youth Leader Tip

A typical junior-higher's picture of church often equals his or her picture of God. A game that you play with your students (such as the one above) can often tell them more about the life and vitality of relationship with God than your well-planned talk!

grain between one's hands was considered threshing; thus it was considered work.

In Luke 6:3-4, we see that Jesus referred them to the biblical story in which David and his men, famished by running from Saul's army, ate the holy bread, breaking the rule against desecrating the bread dedicated to the Lord (see 1 Samuel 21:1-6). Jesus' point was that sometimes, ceremonial rules must give way to more pressing needs such as hunger or healing.

Now ask a volunteer to read Exodus 20:8-9, and then ask, *What was the purpose for the Sabbath?* (To keep it holy, to worship God, and to rest.) Point out that the Jewish leaders and teachers of the Law had gotten so caught up in obeying the letter of the law that they had forgotten that the intent of the law was to set aside time to worship God.

Conclude by explaining that what Jesus did in Luke 6:6-11 is just another example of His placing true needs over the man-made rules for the Sabbath. With the Pharisees watching and waiting to catch Him breaking a rule, Jesus purposely healed a man's crippled hand. He made it clear that helping the man was more important to God than obeying the man-made law and allowing the man to suffer. It is ironic—or perhaps by design—that Jesus was doing good while the Pharisees were plotting evil against Jesus on this Sabbath day (see v. 11; Mark 3:6).

Option 2: Don't Blink. You need nothing but a steely gaze.

Explain that God made some rules for people in the Old Testament to protect their relationships with Him, to keep them wholly devoted to Him and to keep them pure. Let's pretend that God gave this rule: *In order to grow in your relationship with Me, you cannot blink for any reason. As long as you don't blink, you can have a close relationship with Me.*

Ask all of the students to participate and see who can last the longest without blinking. Afterward, ask students what was on their minds the most: their relationship with God or how to keep their eyes open?

Explain that while obviously God didn't give a rule in the Old Testament that you can't blink, some of the Jews in Bible times started focusing on the rules instead of their relationship with God. People mixed man-made rules with God's laws, causing them to be so focused on obeying the rules that they forgot the purpose of the rules to begin with, which was to protect their relationships with God and to help them grow closer to Him.

Ask for a volunteer to read Luke 6:1-11 aloud, and then share the background and contextual information found in Option 1. Once you have finished, discuss the following questions:

1. Did Jesus respect the rules in the Old Testament? *Yes, He obeyed them perfectly, but He knew that the original purpose of God's rules was not being honored.*

2. Did He come to get rid of the rules in the Old Testament (see Matthew 5:17-18)? *No, He came to fulfill every aspect of God's laws, to help us understand what the rules were really meant to do, to protect us and to help our relationships with God grow.*

3. Why didn't Jesus just wait a day and avoid the whole Sabbath controversy? *Because He wanted to show that helping others was more important than following man-made rules; if He had waited, the rule would have seemed more important.*

4. What did it cost Jesus to place the needs of others ahead of the man-made rules of the Sabbath? *Some of the Jews began to plot against Him, which eventually led to His crucifixion. It is ironic, or perhaps by design, that Jesus did good while the Pharisees were plotting evil against Jesus on this Sabbath day (see Luke 6:11; Mark 3:6). So, basically, doing good cost Him His life—but He knew all along that saving us would cost Him His life.*

DIG

Option 1: School Rules. You need enough copies of "School Rules" (found on the next page, as well as on *The Life of Jesus* DVD) for small groups of four to six students, and pens or pencils.

Divide students into groups of four to six; then ask students to name some of the many kinds of rules that they are expected to obey (e.g., school rules, social rules, etiquette rules, religious rules, God's laws, traffic laws, federal laws). Then ask them to give examples of each type of rule or law.

Then explain that while we might not face religious rules the same way Jesus did, there are some rules (for instance, social rules) that govern the way students act at school. Explain that you're not referring to official rules such as not

SCHOOL RULES

Take a few minutes to come up with as many unofficial rules, or expectations, as you can that govern the way you act and who you hang out with at school.

The popular way to dress these days is . . .

_____
_____
_____
_____
_____
_____
_____

The popular things to do after school are . . .

_____
_____
_____
_____
_____
_____

The popular words are . . .

_____
_____
_____
_____
_____
_____
_____
_____
_____
_____
_____
_____

SCHOOL
XING

bringing weapons to school or not cheating—which are rules that absolutely should not be broken.

There are rules about how we treat others, such as who we should hang out with and how we should dress. Although these rules may not seem as important as official rules or God's laws, we suffer the consequences when we don't follow these social rules. We might be teased, declared unpopular or called names if we don't obey them. Different schools and different groups within the school might have different rules.

Distribute "School Rules" and pens or pencils and allow a few minutes for the groups to complete handouts. Then ask each small group to share a few of its answers. Next, discuss the following:

- When would you break these rules?
- What would happen to you if you did?
- What would other people think of you?
- How do you treat those who might not know these rules or expectations or don't follow them?
- When you think about Jesus, who put human needs over others' expectations and rules, what do you think He would want you to do?

Option 2: When Breaking the Rules Is a Good Idea. You need this tricky case study and some wise students.

Read the following case study and use the questions that follow to illustrate when breaking a rule is necessary to help someone:

Lisa and Kristin have been best friends since fourth grade. They know everything about each other. They know all about each other's family problems, secret crushes and insecurities.

One day Lisa made Kristin promise not to tell anyone her secret, which Kristin immediately promised. But imagine her great shock when Lisa told her she wanted to kill herself. "Don't tell *anyone*," Lisa urged, "but I'm so tired of my life. My mom would throw a fit if she knew."

Kristin doesn't know what to do. She did her best to talk Lisa out of her decision, but Lisa had made up her mind. "You promised you wouldn't tell," Lisa reminded her friend. Kristin knew she would never forgive herself if Lisa went through with it and actually killed herself. She knew the rule of friendship—always keep a secret—but she also knew that obeying that rule in this case could cost Lisa her life.

Discuss the following questions:

- What are Kristin's options?
- What might be the consequences of Kristen telling Lisa's secret?
- What might be the consequences of Kristen keeping Lisa's secret?
- In this case, should the rules be broken?
- What if Kristin loses Lisa's friendship in the process of helping her?

The truth is, Kristin could lose her friend whether or not she breaks their rule and tells someone of Lisa's plan. But whether Lisa forgives her for telling or not, at least Lisa will be alive to make that choice.

APPLY

Option 1: The Top Two. You need your Bible, enough copies of "The Top Two" (found on the next page and on *The Life of Jesus* DVD) for each student, and pens or pencils.

Ask for a volunteer to read Matthew 22:34-40, and then explain that once again, the Pharisees were trying to trick Jesus regarding the rules, but Jesus had a simple answer. Ask students how they would put Jesus' answer in their own words. Clarify that Jesus obeyed these two rules above *all* others. These two rules are the basis of all the other rules.

Distribute "The Top Two" and pens and pencils. Ask students to take their time and really think about their answers. Allow several minutes for students to complete the handout; then invite some of them to discuss their answers with the whole group.

Close in prayer, asking God to help each person be a great example of Jesus' top two rules.

Youth Leader Tip
One of the most effective ways for teaching students how to commune with God is to let them overhear your prayers. As often as you feel comfortable, pray aloud in your group. Keep in mind, though, that a junior-higher's attention span is short—so avoid long prayers.

THE TOP TWO

Jesus gives us two big rules in Matthew 22:34-40: (1) Love God above all else, and (2) Love your neighbor as yourself. Complete the following statements:

One thing I'm doing that is helping me to love God is . . .

_____
_____
_____
_____

One thing I'm doing that is making it harder for me to love God is . . .

_____
_____
_____
_____

One thing I'm doing that is helping me to love others is . . .

_____
_____
_____
_____

One thing I'm doing that is making it harder for me to love others is . . .

_____
_____
_____
_____

After thinking about my answers above, one thing I'd like to do differently is . . .

_____
_____
_____
_____

Option 2: Church Rules. You need some creative students, a whiteboard and a dry-erase marker.

Suggest that some people don't come to church because they see it as a place with a bunch of rules, and that isn't very much fun. Read Matthew 22:34-40 aloud and then explain that Jesus names two big rules here. What are they? (*Love God above all else* and *love each other.*) Write these on the board when students come up with them.

Then ask students to brainstorm some ideas for how you all can make the group reflect more of the way you love God and love others. Ideas might include doing a better job greeting guests, contacting guests in the next week or having food at every meeting (a junior high favorite!). Write their suggestions on the whiteboard.

Now ask them to name some ideas for how to show others that they do more at church than just talk about everything that God doesn't want them to do. Write those suggestions on the whiteboard, too, which may include playing more games, singing more rowdy songs and having food (note the food theme here).

If students come up with lots of ideas, you might want to ask them to vote to narrow it down to the most important ways you can love God and others and have fun while doing it! Close by inviting volunteers who would like to help make any of the ideas happen to come talk with you before they leave.

REFLECT

The following short devotions are for the students to reflect on and answer during the week. You can make a copy of these pages and distribute to your class or print out from the PDF for this session found on *The Life of Jesus* DVD.

1—DIFFICULT DECISION

Read 1 John 2:15-17 and ask yourself, *Do I have an expiration date like a bag of chips?*

Christmas vacation was just around the corner! Josh was totally excited—two weeks of sleeping late, no homework and doing whatever it was that he wanted to do.

On the last day of classes before break, Paul, Josh's friend from youth group, ran up to him in the lunchroom and said, "I've got great news! There's another spot on that mission trip to help the homeless in the inner city next week. Do you still want to go?"

Josh's other friend, Bill, overheard them and laughed as he remarked, "What a way to waste your vacation!"

Sometimes the world considers helping others foolish or unimportant. You may find yourself having to choose which is more important—doing what God wants you to do for other people or doing what the world says you should do for yourself.

Have you ever found yourself in a situation like Josh's? What did you do in that particular situation?

_____

_____

_____

_____

_____

What is one way that you can serve God and others more today?

_____

_____

_____

_____

_____

2—HOW WOULD YOU FEEL?

Hey! What are you doing? Go read Matthew 8:9-12!

Imagine you're a homeless person sitting on a sidewalk, begging for food or spare change. How would you feel if someone . . .

- Gave you a can of lima beans?
- Laughed at you and kicked your feet?
- Gave you 14 pennies?
- Called you lazy and worthless?
- Gave you a sandwich and offered to take you to a local shelter?

When you look at someone who needs help, do you remember how much God loves both of you?

_____
_____
_____
_____

Do you let God use you to help others, despite what other people might think?

_____
_____
_____
_____

What's one thing that you can do to serve someone else today?

_____
_____
_____
_____

3—GOD IS GOOD

Read Mark 7:8 and hold on!

Tina was what everyone called a "good girl." She did well in school, obeyed her parents, and saved her money. She didn't cuss, and she always kept her room neat and clean. She kept away from the kids in the bad crowd and made fun of them with her friends, knowing that she and her friends were better than those losers.

One weekend, she went with her friend Kalifa on a youth group retreat. She became a Christian that week and realized that even though everyone said she was good, God had a different standard for how she had to behave. She went home confused and a little scared about the ways that she needed to change her life.

It's easy to get distracted by what people tell you is the right way to behave. God wants you to understand that you are supposed to be listening to what *He* tells you is good, not what other people tell you.

Are you paying attention to what the world says or to what God says is good? Pray right now and ask Him for the strength to follow His will for your life instead of what the world says you should do.

4—SMARTY PANTS

Hey! Flip to 1 Corinthians 1:18-19 as fast as you can.

How smart do you think these decisions are? Check the smartest:

- ☐ Dropping out of school to become a clown
- ☐ Throwing coleslaw out your window
- ☐ Paying $50 to go on a missions trip without showers or flush toilets
- ☐ Dancing around yelling, "I'm a butterfly! I'm a butterfly!"

Sometimes God tells us to do one thing when the world tells us it's stupid.

Why is the cross foolish to some people?

_____

_____

_____

_____

What's one way you can tell others about how God makes sense to you?

_____

_____

_____

_____

What do you have to lose if you tell others about God?

_____

_____

_____

_____

_____

What do you have to gain?

_____

_____

_____

_____

_____

THE BIGGEST ONE

THE BIG IDEA
You can believe in the greatest miracle since creation: Jesus' resurrection!

SESSION AIMS
In this session you will guide students to (1) understand the depth of Jesus' love and sacrifice for each of them; (2) experience the power of the resurrection and how it can dramatically change their lives; and (3) be transformed and find ways to share this truth with others.

THE BIGGEST VERSE
"But these are written that you may believe that Jesus is the Christ, the Son of God, and that by believing you may have life in his name" (John 20:31).

OTHER IMPORTANT VERSES
Matthew 28:8; John 11:25; 20:1-31; Romans 10:9-10; 1 Corinthians 15:13-14; 2 Corinthians 5:20; Colossians 3:13

STARTER

Option 1: Which Is Worse? For this option, you will just need the following list of questions.

Greet students and let them know that today it's their turn to give you their opinions! Read the following statements one at a time, explaining that if they think the first option would be worse, they should go to the right wall; if the second option would be worse, they should go to the left wall.

Ask: *Which is worse?*

- To have your hair fall out for a month or to lose the use of your fingers for two weeks?
- To miss your favorite TV show or not to listen to a radio for a week?
- To have your math homework accidentally go down the garbage disposal or to lose your retainer?
- To miss your allowance for a month or to lose your favorite jacket?
- To have your nose disappear or to have your ears become invisible?
- To lose your skateboard or to lose your bike?
- To have your fingers disappear or to have your toes disappear?
- To lose your mp3 player or to lose your favorite computer game?

Now discuss the following:

1. What do all of these things have in common? *They all refer to something that is missing.*

2. Have you ever lost something or had something go missing? How did you feel?

Explain that once in history, something was missing, but instead of being bad news, it was the greatest news of all time. You might not have heard about it yet, but by the end of this session, you will.

Option 2: What Is Missing? You need adult volunteers, candy prizes and a room that has a lot of objects in it. (If your room is a bit sparse, you might want to bring some objects from home: books, papers, trinkets, and so forth.)

Greet students and divide them into two teams. Let them know that you want to test their powers of observation. Explain the exercise: They are going to close their eyes and you will walk around and remove one item from its place in the room. When you put that item out of sight, you'll instruct students to open their eyes.

The first person to figure out what's missing should raise her hand. If she is right, her team gets 1,000 points. If she is wrong, her team loses 500 points and the other team gets to guess. Ask adult volunteers to walk around the room while you remove the item to make sure no one sneaks a look. Deduct 2,000 points from the team of anyone caught peeking. Just to make sure, you might want to have students put their heads down and cover their closed eyes with their hands. If you have enough blindfolds, by all means, use them!

Play three to five rounds of the game (depending on the amount of time you have and whether or not you need a tiebreaker); then award candy to the winning team. Then discuss the following:

- Have you ever lost something? How did you feel?
- What did you do to try to find it?
- How did you feel when you found it?

Explain that once in history, something was missing, but instead of being bad news, it was the greatest news of all time. You might not have heard about it yet, but by the end of this session, you will.

MESSAGE

Option 1: Inside and Outside. You need several Bibles, lots of old magazines and newspapers, glue, enough scissors for every three to five students to share a pair, paper lunch bags, construction paper and pens.

Divide students into groups of three to five and give each group several magazines, newspapers, pens and some construction paper. Distribute a paper bag and one or more pairs of scissors to each group as you explain the exercise: Each student's paper bag represents him or her. Students are to use the magazines and newspapers to find words or pictures that relate to how people view them, and then glue those words or pictures to the *outside* of the bag. For example, if someone is viewed as an athlete, he or she might find a ball or a word that describes athletes.

On the *inside* of the bag, students are to place (*not glue!*) pictures or words that symbolize something about them that *people may not know*. For example, if someone loves vegetables, skateboards on the weekends or maybe even sings in the shower, he or she might find a picture or word that illustrates those components of who he or she is. If students can't find a specific word or picture that tells a particular aspect about them, they can use the construction paper and pens to write or draw that characteristic.

Allow 10 minutes for students to construct their Image Bags. Then invite those who would like to share theirs with the whole group to do so.

Point out that it can be difficult to share hidden secrets about ourselves, partly because people are skeptical. God sent Jesus as a sacrifice for the sins of humanity. Jesus attempted many times to explain this hidden truth to those who followed Him, but they, too, were skeptical. Many of His followers still did not believe until His resurrection actually occurred.

Next, read John 20:1-31 around the group (each student reads a verse, with the student to his or her right reading the next one; continue until the passage is completed). Ask students to look through the magazines and newspapers again, but this time to look for things that describe how people viewed Jesus on the outside and who He was on the inside. No gluing is necessary this time; just ask students to gather what they can. Allow two minutes or so for students to gather information; then ask for volunteers to show what they've chosen and explain why they chose those things.

Use the following information to help in explaining the John 20 passage to students:

In John 20:2, when Mary Magdalene ran to find Peter and John, the leaders of the disciples, she tells them, "They have taken the Lord." Although she never mentions who "they" are, she was referring to the authorities who were behind Jesus' death. The quick response of Peter and John in verses 3 and 4 indicates that the disciples were not responsible for removing the body.[1]

In John 20:6-7, Peter sees "strips of linen" and a "burial cloth," which is a cloth that had been around Jesus' head. Peter was possibly wondering why the clothes were left so neatly if grave robbers had

Youth Leader Tip

Collect magazines for learning activities such as the one above or for sprucing up posters, signs or bulletin boards. Hang on to the ones you buy or have students bring them in. One caution: Check through magazines first for objectionable content. A little discretion will go a long way!

taken the body. In fact, he might have been thinking: *Why would a robber have taken the clothes off of Jesus' body in the first place?*

When the angels are described in John 20:12, all we learn is that they were clothed in white. When angels are mentioned in the Bible, they are usually recognized by their powers, not by any significant difference from human form.

In verses 14-16, Mary finally recognized Jesus when He said one simple word—her name, Mary.

Jesus doesn't seem to be stopped by locked doors (see v. 19). There was a similarity between His resurrection body and His human body since He still had scars that identified Him; but since humans can't walk through locked doors (you'll probably get hurt if you try this at home), His resurrection body is definitely different.

Even though Jesus wasn't present when Thomas expressed his doubts to the other disciples (see vv. 24-25), Jesus knew that Thomas had doubted. Jesus commended Thomas, but also commended those who haven't seen Him and yet believe in Him. (That includes us!) Also, note that Thomas was the first to declare "My Lord and my God" (v. 28). Jesus answered Thomas in a way that left no doubt in his mind who Jesus was!

Conclude by discussing the following questions:

- What are some words you would add to your descriptions of Jesus?
- If you were the apostles, why might you have not believed Jesus' words?
- Is there any part of the Resurrection story that is difficult for you to understand?
- In what ways might you relate to the apostles' lack of understanding and weak faith?

Option 2: My Obituary. You need your Bible, enough copies of "My Obituary" (found on the next page and on *The Life of Jesus* DVD) for everyone, and pens or pencils. You also might want to cut out an obituary page from a newspaper in case students are unfamiliar with an obituary.

Begin by asking students to explain what an obituary is. If no one knows, show your example and explain that an obituary is a recording of someone's life and death. It's often found in newspapers or magazines and highlights the life of the deceased.

✝ My Obituary

What would you like to leave as your mark on this earth if you had only the next five years to do it? How would you want to be remembered?

Biographical information:

_____
_____
_____
_____
_____
_____
_____
_____
_____
_____

Your hobbies and interests:

_____
_____
_____
_____
_____
_____
_____
_____
_____
_____

People you spent time with:

_____
_____
_____
_____
_____
_____
_____
_____
_____
_____

Things you accomplished:

_____
_____
_____
_____
_____
_____
_____
_____
_____
_____

Distribute "My Obituary" and pens or pencils. Instruct students to write a fake obituary about themselves—writing as if the obituary were dated five years from now. They should think about what they would want people to know about them and the way they lived their lives, their accomplishments, their loyalties, and so forth. Allow a few minutes for students to write; then invite willing students to share what they wrote.

Explain that before the Son of God was born a baby in Bethlehem, He knew how His obituary would read. He knew that He was being sent to earth by His Father to die for the sins of the world. He knew that there would be many who wouldn't believe. He also knew that His followers, those who would witness the greatest miracle in history, His resurrection, would be responsible for telling others about Him. He knew that it would be up to us as His followers to continue to spread the news of His great love to the whole world.

Read John 20:1-31 aloud; then discuss:

- Who do you think that you would have been most like in the story: excited-but-scared Mary Magdalene, fearful John, curious Peter or doubting Thomas?

- Which person in the story is most like your friends at school?

- If you had been Mary Magdalene, what questions might you have wanted to ask Jesus?

DIG

Option 1: Not Like Santa Claus. You need some Christmas music and a way to play it for everyone.

Play the Christmas music in the background to set the mood as you ask how many of the students still believe in Santa Claus. (Don't expect many hands to go up! If they do say they still believe, you're in trouble now for bursting their bubble!) Then ask if anyone knows if Santa Claus was a real person. If no one knows, explain that there was a real person who was a priest known as Saint Nicholas. This man gave gifts to poor children and was generally an all-around good guy. Many legends have grown up about Saint Nicholas, which have since developed into the present-day legend of Santa Claus.

Next, point out that some people think of Jesus in the same way they think of Santa Claus: that He was just a really good person whose story has become an exaggerated work of fiction—a legend. Then discuss the following:

1. How does Jesus' life differ from that of Saint Nicholas? *Jesus' life hasn't become larger than life—His life, His death and His resurrection are very real and, unlike Saint Nicholas, He lives today.*

2. Why is belief in the Resurrection so important to being a Christian? *Because if the promises Jesus made concerning His resurrection and our own are false, then there is no hope (see 1 Corinthians 15:13-14).*

3. What makes someone a Christian? *Believing that Jesus is Lord, that He died on the cross for our sins, that He was raised from the dead and that He lives today (see Romans 10:9-10). Because of these truths, we have eternal life with God.*

Option 2: What Hope Means. For this option, you will need a whiteboard and a dry-erase marker. Begin by reading the following case study:

Melissa is a confident eighth grader who always seems to take control. She is student-body president at her school, chairman of the social committee in her youth group, and an honor student. Walking home from school one day, she was surprised to see her mother's car in front of the house. She ran in to find her mother crumpled on the couch, crying. Melissa's pastor was there in an attempt to comfort Melissa's mom. Melissa found out that her father had been killed in a car accident just two hours before.

Ask students what Jesus might want Melissa and her mom to know that could comfort them. (Because Jesus was resurrected, believers too have the hope of eternal life through Him. In John 11:25, Jesus said, "I am the resurrection and the life. He who believes in me will live, even though he dies; and whoever lives and believes in me will never die.")

Youth Leader Tip

Whenever possible, allow students to be part of the creative process during the meeting time. Allowing them to post artwork or create skits will give them possession of the meeting room or group time and create an environment of safety, acceptance, fun and celebration.

Using the board to record their answers, asks students to brainstorm some ways that Jesus' resurrection affects our lives. Then ask how the Resurrection *should* affect our everyday lives.

APPLY

Option 1: Jesus Graffiti. For this option, you will need several gift Bibles, paper, pens or pencils, a large piece of foam-core board or stiff cardboard, brick-colored paint, spray paint (or large felt-tip pens or acrylic paints and brushes if you are reluctant to let your group get their hands on spray paint!) and several rectangular sponges.

Have students take turns dipping the sponges into the paint and applying it to the face of the cardboard in a brick design, until it resembles a large brick wall. Next, allow students to spray paint their names on the board in one color. After all are done, spray paint the name "JESUS" onto the board.

Explain that if this board represented history, their names would correspond to all the great leaders and historical figures we've ever had on earth. Jesus overshadowed all of these great leaders in one action: His resurrection. Jesus was a good man, but so were many others in history. He was a good teacher, but so were many that preceded Him. That He rose from the dead puts Him above all others. Not one of the others has done that!

Continue by explaining that Jesus indeed changed history, but the history He's most interested in is each of ours. He wants to redeem us from the sin in our history and prepare a future for us with Him. He wants us to make Him our Savior by rescuing us from our sin and taking over our lives.

But being our Savior isn't enough for Jesus; He also wants to be our Lord. Some of us have asked Jesus to take control of our lives but still struggle with letting Him really be Lord over everything we do and say.

Have students bow their heads and ask them to keep their eyes closed. If there is anyone who would like to ask Jesus to be their Savior for the first time, invite them to raise their hand.

Wait a moment for hands to be raised, and then invite anyone who has already asked Jesus to be their Savior, but still has areas of his or life in which he or she struggles to make Him Lord, to raise his or her hand.

Close in prayer, asking students to repeat a simple prayer of dedication after you: *Dear Jesus, I believe that You rose from the dead and that You are alive now. I need You to take over my life and forgive me of my sin. Help me to make You my Savior and my Lord. Amen.*

MY LIFE, MY CIRCLE

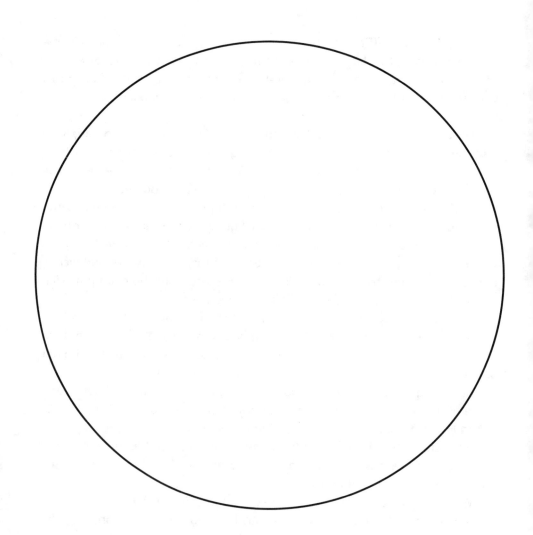

Invite all who raised their hands to see you before they leave so that you can give them a gift. Give each of those who responded a gift Bible as they leave, making sure that you get the names, addresses, phone numbers and email addresses of everyone who has made a new commitment to Jesus. Contact them within a week to encourage them and invite them back to church.

Option 2: My Life, My Circle. You need several gift Bibles, enough copies of "My Life, My Circle" (found on the preceeding page and on *The Life of Jesus* DVD) for everyone, pens or pencils, several pairs of scissors and a pie tin.

Distribute "My Life, My Circle" and pens or pencils, then ask if anyone knows what a pie chart is. (It's a circle shape divided into sections like pie pieces with each section representing a percentage of the whole circle. The larger the percentage, the bigger the piece.)

Explain that the circle on the handout represents their lives. Ask them to designate a section that represents how much of their lives they've given over to God; then divide the rest of the circle into other pieces, based on the number and importance of other things that take up their lives.

Allow a few minutes for working on the handout; then distribute scissors and invite students to cut out any pieces of the pie that they would like to get rid of. Have them come forward and place those pieces into the pie tin as a sign that they want Jesus to be in control of all their lives.

Close in prayer, thanking God for His incredible faithfulness to us and ask Him to help students to allow Jesus to be their Lord and Savior, taking over every aspect of their lives. *Note:* If some of your students have not yet asked Jesus to be their Savior, you can incorporate the last portion of Option 1 to lead them through the prayer, asking Him to come into their lives. This is where the gift Bibles come in handy!

REFLECT

The following short devotions are for the students to reflect on and answer during the week. You can make a copy of these pages and distribute to your class or print out from the PDF for this session found on *The Life of Jesus* DVD.

1—NEW PEOPLE

Try to find 1 Peter 1:3-5 with your eyes closed.

Last year, Danny was an average eighth grader. He liked to listen to music, ride his skateboard and hang out with his friends. Like all of his friends, Danny complained about his parents and his teachers and liked to talk about girls, video games and movies. Sometimes he got in trouble when he failed a test or his mom heard him cussing, but overall he was a typical teen.

This year—*wow!*—Danny is different. He became a Christian over the summer and now he tells everyone at school about Jesus and the cross and how totally amazing it was when Jesus was resurrected. It's as if Danny were a whole new person!

When we accept Jesus into our hearts, we become new people. That's how amazing Jesus' death and resurrection are!

Think of one person you can tell today about the amazing thing Jesus did for you.

2—REALLY BIG GIFT

Go to Romans 5:6-8 for a demonstration.

How would you feel if your best friend in the whole world . . .

- Gave you the pudding cup from his or her lunch?
- Let you wear his or her favorite sweatshirt all winter?
- Threw a giant surprise party for you?
- Let you have all the money in his or her piggy bank?

Do you know that God loved you so much that He was willing to give up the One who meant the most to Him—His own Son? He did it in order to show you how much He loves and cares for you. Thank God for this totally amazing gift today!

What is one way that you can show this type of love and care to someone else in your life today?

_____

_____

_____

_____

_____

3—GET CHANGED

Get up and read Romans 6:3-4.

Tina has changed so much in the last few months. She's telling everyone she runs into about Jesus, even at her Christian middle school! She's been volunteering at the hospital and telling everyone there about what Jesus did for the world on the cross. The funny thing is that Tina has been calling herself a Christian for many years, but only just now does she realize how incredible God's gift to her through Jesus is.

How cool is it to realize that God has given you new life? It's so amazing that you have to change when you realize it's true!

Thank God for sending His Son to be a sacrifice for your sins. Ask Him to show you a way that you can be changed by Him today.

4—SPIRITUAL GIFT

Look up 1 John 4:13-16 and learn about a gift you've been given.

Merry Christmas! Under the tree, you have left your favorite cousin a present. What's under the shiny wrapping paper and big bow?

- ❏ A package of broken crackers from under your bed
- ❏ Your dirty laundry for him to fluff and fold
- ❏ You old worn-out sneakers that you got as a present last year
- ❏ Your collection of empty soda cans
- ❏ Your love (how did you get that into a box anyway?)

When Jesus went up to heaven, He gave us a gift that would be with us always—the Holy Spirit.

What kind of place does the Holy Spirit have in your life?

_____

_____

_____

_____

_____

How might your day be different if you remember that the Holy Spirit lives in-side of you today?

_____

_____

_____

_____

_____

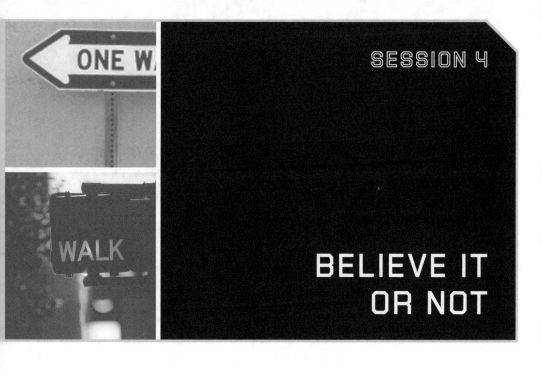

BELIEVE IT OR NOT

THE BIG IDEA

Your faith is often part of the healing process.

SESSION AIMS

In this session you will guide students to (1) understand that faith can play a huge role in their healing; (2) feel the power of God in their lives; and (3) act by expressing their faith in God this week.

THE BIGGEST VERSE

"When she heard about Jesus, she came up behind him in the crowd and touched his cloak, because she thought, 'If I just touch his clothes, I will be healed'" (Mark 5:27-28).

OTHER IMPORTANT VERSES

Leviticus 12:1-8; 15:19-30; Mark 2:1-12; 5:25-34; 9:14-32; Hebrews 2:9-18; 11:1

STARTER

Option 1: Bubble-lympics. You need two adult volunteers, oodles and oodles of the same-sized but different-colored bubble gum (each team of 10 students will need 30 pieces of gum in its team's color), a hula-hoop, a tarp, masking tape, two rulers and a Barbie-type doll (or other doll with hair) for each team. *Note:* The dolls should be ones you don't want to keep afterward, because they'll be a little sticky!

Ahead of time, place the tarp in an open area, place the hula-hoop in the middle of the tarp and use the masking tape to mark a very wide line three feet from the tarp.

At the meeting, greet students and divide them into teams of fewer than 10 students each. Let them know that they're going to compete in the "Bubble-lympics" and assign each team a color corresponding to the colors of bubble gum you have. (If you don't have enough colors of gum, ask teams to take two halves of different colored gum and make their own color, i.e., grape and cherry, or apple and watermelon.)

Distribute a piece of the appropriately colored gum to each team member and announce the first game in the Bubble-lympics: Basket-Bubble. Instruct them to start chewing as you explain the rules: Each team must line up at one end of the room, opposite the tarp and hula-hoop. On your signal, the first team members in each line will run toward the tarp and spit their gum into the hoop from *behind* the tape line. Then they run back and tag the next person in line; this continues until each team member has taken their shot.

Each piece of gum that lands inside the hoop will earn its team 1,000 points (see why you need different colors?). The team that finishes first gets an additional 4,000 points.

Total the points and transition to the second event: Hair Sculpting. Give each team member another piece of his or her team's gum, and then give each team a doll. Explain the rules: Using all your team's gum, teammates must sculpt Barbie's hair into a new style. The most creative and/or best style will earn 10,000 points and the second-place team will get 7,000 points (and so on, if you have more than two teams).

Total up the points and move on to the final event: Bubble-Blow. Have each team send up three representatives and give each of them another piece of their team's gum. Explain the rules: This one's easy. All you have to do is blow the biggest bubble you can and hold it as long as you can without popping it! Ask the adult volunteers to be ready with their rulers to measure the size of the bubbles before they pop! Choose the five best bubble blowers (or 10, depending on how big the group is) to remain and compete in the final round of Bubble-Blow. Award 10,000 points for the biggest bubble; award 7,000 points for second place, and so on. Next, discuss the following questions:

1. Did everyone who competed have the same amount of gum to start with? *Yes.*

2. Did the amount of gum have anything to do with who blew the biggest bubble? *No, because everyone had the same amount.*

3. What made the difference between the winner and the losers? *Answers may include strategy, luck, big mouth, extra hot air, skill, and so forth.*

Conclude by explaining that just as everyone who competed started out with the same amount of gum, God's awesome power is always the same. Why then do some people tend to see more of God's power (or in terms of our game, bigger bubbles) while others see less? It doesn't take strategy or luck or practice; what it does take is something called faith. Hebrews 11:1 defines faith as "being sure of what we hope for and certain of what we do not see." You're going to check out God's unchanging power today.

Option 2: Name That Noise. You need an adult volunteer, a stopwatch, an audio recorder and a way to play your recordings.

Ahead of time, record 10 seconds of sound from a variety of appliances (e.g., refrigerator, dishwasher, hair dryer, microwave, blender, mixer, dryer, washer, halogen lamp). Be sure to write down the names of what you record so that you'll know if students identify sounds correctly!

At the meeting, greet students and then divide them into two teams (or more if the group is larger than 20 students). Explain that you're going to play Name That Noise! Set up the player and have the adult volunteer be ready with the stopwatch.

Ask for a representative from each team and start the bidding by asking one of the team reps: *In how many seconds can your team Name That Noise!?* Allow him to answer; then ask the opposing team rep if she thinks her team can do it faster. Continue the bidding back and forth until the teams reach a standoff; then challenge the team whose rep bid the least amount of time to Name That Noise! Have the adult volunteer count down from 3 seconds, and then press "play" on the player. When the volunteer calls time, press "stop." (Be prepared for students to bid as low as .5 seconds or .25 seconds as they get competitive. Only allow this if your stopwatch has that function.) Give the lowest bidding team a few seconds to discuss their answer and then make their guess.

If they correctly identify the noise, award the team 10,000 points; if they can't name it in the allotted amount of time, subtract 7,000 points and give the opposing team the opportunity to guess (without playing the recording again). Continue the process until you've run out of noises or when students get restless or bored.

Discuss the following:

1. What's one thing all these noises have in common? *They're all from appliances.*

2. What is one thing that all the appliances have in common? *They all need electricity.*

3. What happens when these aren't plugged in? *They won't work because they need power.*

Explain that in order to understand God more fully, we must stay plugged in to His power and have faith that His power will work. Hebrews 11:1 defines faith as "being sure of what we hope for and certain of what we do not see." Today you're going to learn more about what that means.

MESSAGE

Option 1: Yum or Yuck. You need two adult volunteers, two pieces of cardboard, a marker, two blindfolds, and a myriad of canned, dried and fresh foods (some of these should be pretty odd, but we don't recommend sardines or anything that might taste too gross).

Youth Leader Tip

If your junior-highers are like most, they will tend to remember things that are active and more visual. The more that you can add action to your youth talks—whether they do the action or watch it—the more information they will ultimately retain.

Ahead of time, use the cardboard and marker to make two signs: one that reads "Yum" and another that reads "Yuck." Also arrange for the adult volunteers to hold up the signs during the exercise and signal the audience to react to what each sign signifies. The "Yum" sign holder will hold up his sign each time Taste Tester One takes a bite; the "Yuck" sign holder will do the same for Taste Tester Two.

At the meeting, ask for two volunteers who are not afraid to eat some strange foods. Explain that none of the foods will make them sick (hopefully!), but some of it probably won't be found on their plate every day. Once you have two taste testers, blindfold them and explain that this exercise will test their faith and confidence in you, because you're the one who chose the food. Ask the taste testers to hold their noses while you give them each bites of different foods. They won't be able to see or smell what you're feeding them.

Begin feeding the different foods to the guinea pigs (oops, we mean taste testers). Cue the sign holders to do their jobs and get the audience to react to what you're feeding the taste testers.

When they're done, ask the taste testers:

- How did you feel when you were eating the foods?
- How did what the audience said affect you?
- Why did you act the way you did?

Ask the audience what they think this exercise has to do with faith. (The tasters were sent mixed signals and had to decide if their faith in the person who chose the food was stronger than the signals they got from the audience.) Then tell the students that today you're going to study a woman who was sent some mixed signals but responded with faith. Read Mark 5:25-34, adding the following contextual information as appropriate:

Scripture doesn't tell us exactly why this woman had been bleeding for so long. It could be that she had some type of uterine disease. Although she had spent all her money and seen many doctors, she wasn't getting any better. To make the situation even more desperate, according to the interpretation of Leviticus 12:1-8 and 15:19-30, as long as she was bleeding, she was ritually unclean.

She also may have held the common superstitious belief that a healer's power was transmitted through his or her clothing. Now this unclean woman who wasn't supposed to touch anyone approached

Jesus from behind, hoping that she would go unnoticed. But Jesus noticed. Healing energy had left Him.

Jesus' disciples thought it was pretty pointless to try to figure out who had touched Him, but Jesus insisted. When He found her, Jesus addressed her as "daughter"—the only time He addresses a woman by that word in all of the Gospels. The word He used is *sesoken* in Greek, which means "has saved."[1] Jesus linked her spiritual salvation with her physical healing.

Connect the story to the food exercise by asking what mixed signals might have been sent to the woman. (She shouldn't touch anyone because she would make whomever she touched unclean; she wasn't worth anything; Jesus was too busy.) Then ask why they think she touched Jesus anyway. (She had so much faith in Him that she knew all she had to do was to touch His garment and He would heal her.)

Option 2: What She Had to Do. You need your Bible and some mobile students.

Read Mark 5:25-34 aloud. Explain that this woman had ultimate faith in Christ's ability to heal her—so much so that she knew all she had to do was to reach out and touch His clothing! Before she could be healed, she had to do three things:

1. *Recognize His power* (see Mark 5:28). Elaborate in this way: *What would happen if I stuck my tongue into a light socket? Even though I have never actually done that, based upon my experiences, training and knowledge, I wouldn't attempt such a stupid thing (well, at least with all of you watching!). Why wouldn't I? Because I have a healthy fear of pain. I know if I were to do that, it would hurt. In a similar way, I have a healthy respect for God's power. Although He has the power to zap me into a little pile of ashes, He loves me enough not to. The bleeding woman understood not only His power to heal but also His love for her.* Illustrate this by asking for a student volunteer to come to the front of the room. Have him flex his muscles, making sure the crowd cheers for him as he does. Explain that whenever you say "Jesus" from now on (you can decide if it's until the end of the lesson, or just until the end of this option), that student has to flex his muscles to remind us of Jesus' power.

2. *Revere Him* (see Mark 5:33). Explain: *The bleeding woman had a healthy respect for the power of Jesus to heal her. When confronted, she bowed down in front of Jesus because of her healthy respect for who He was, which was God. We should approach Him the same way.* Ask for another volunteer who will come to the front of the room. Explain to this volunteer that her job is to bow down whenever you say "Jesus" as a reminder of the woman's reverence for Him.

3. *Reach out for help* (see Mark 5:34). Describe it like this: *Although the saying "God helps those who help themselves" is not in the Bible, there might be a bit of truth to it. This woman took an active role in her healing by bringing the need to Jesus and trusting in His ability to take care of it. She had tried all the doctors she could, but eventually had to trust in Jesus, the Great Physician.* Yep, you guessed it. You need a third volunteer, who will reach up to the sky, as if reaching up to God, when you say "Jesus."

Oh, and by the way: Make sure you say "Jesus" frequently!

DIG

Option 1: Who Do You Go To? You need enough copies of "Who Do You Go To?" (found on the next page and on *The Life of Jesus* DVD) for everyone, and pens or pencils.

Distribute "Who Do You Go To?" and pens or pencils to students. When they have completed the handout, have them share some of their answers either in small groups or with the whole group. Then discuss:

- Who do you trust the most with your secrets and problems?
- Why that person?
- Let's say you have a problem you can't solve—how well would that person be able to help you if you didn't ask for help?
- How much does your faith in that person contribute to your going to him or her?
- How does your answer relate to the way you approach God when you have a secret or problem?
- If you had to rank God's trustworthiness on a scale of 0 to 10 with 10 being the highest, where would you put Him?

WHO DO YOU GO TO?

On a scale of 0 to 10 (0 indicating that you would never go to that person and 10 indicating that you would run and tell that person as quickly as you could) how likely are you to go to the following people if you have a problem?

Your mom or stepmom
| 0 | 1 | 2 | 3 | 4 | 5 | 6 | 7 | 8 | 9 | 10 |

Your dad or stepdad
| 0 | 1 | 2 | 3 | 4 | 5 | 6 | 7 | 8 | 9 | 10 |

Your closest friend
| 0 | 1 | 2 | 3 | 4 | 5 | 6 | 7 | 8 | 9 | 10 |

A friend who is not as close
| 0 | 1 | 2 | 3 | 4 | 5 | 6 | 7 | 8 | 9 | 10 |

A teacher
| 0 | 1 | 2 | 3 | 4 | 5 | 6 | 7 | 8 | 9 | 10 |

A school counselor
| 0 | 1 | 2 | 3 | 4 | 5 | 6 | 7 | 8 | 9 | 10 |

A neighbor
| 0 | 1 | 2 | 3 | 4 | 5 | 6 | 7 | 8 | 9 | 10 |

An aunt or uncle
| 0 | 1 | 2 | 3 | 4 | 5 | 6 | 7 | 8 | 9 | 10 |

A cousin
| 0 | 1 | 2 | 3 | 4 | 5 | 6 | 7 | 8 | 9 | 10 |

An adult at church
| 0 | 1 | 2 | 3 | 4 | 5 | 6 | 7 | 8 | 9 | 10 |

- Why would you put Him there?
- Where do you wish you would put Him?

Note: Encourage students to be honest with their answers to these questions instead of telling you what they think you want to hear. You might want to set a tone for vulnerability by explaining that God on your continuum probably isn't a 10 (unless it is, in which case you're pretty much a saint and maybe should be writing this book yourself!).

Option 2: "Unanswered" Prayer. You need the synapses in your brain to be working really well for this one.

Read the following case study:

Karissa has always been a good Christian. She goes to church every Sunday, reads her Bible most nights a week before she goes to bed, and tries not to swear too much. She even takes care of her little brothers and sisters when her dad is late getting home from work.

But Karissa has one major problem: Her mom has breast cancer. It's really bad. She has already had chemotherapy and radiation, but it doesn't seem to be helping. She keeps getting weaker and weaker. Karissa, her dad and the rest of the kids pray for her, but she doesn't seem to get any better.

One Wednesday morning, her mother dies. That afternoon, the youth pastor goes over to the house to comfort the family. Karissa's 11-year-old brother asks her, "Why did our mom die, even though we prayed for her a lot? I thought Jesus promised to answer our prayers."

Now discuss the following questions:

1. What would you say if you were the youth pastor?

2. Have you ever prayed for something and even believed God could do it, but it didn't come true?

3. Why do you think God sometimes doesn't answer our prayers, even though we have faith? *We often think of God as a spiritual slot machine: If we do a certain thing, we'll get a blessing in return. He is much more complex than that and knows everything about our situation. His*

will might be for someone not to get healed because He can use something about that illness to help others come to know Him. After all, if knowing Jesus is the most important thing in the world, then anything that happens to us, no matter how painful, can be good if it helps us and others come to know Jesus.

APPLY

Option 1: Help My Unbelief. You need several Bibles, enough copies of "Help My Unbelief" (found on the next page and on *The Life of Jesus* DVD) for everyone, and pens or pencils.

Explain that often we have *some* faith, but maybe not as much as we'd like. Read Mark 9:14-32 aloud and then ask students how much faith the boy's dad had. What did he do to increase his faith? (He asked Jesus to help him.)

Distribute "Help My Unbelief" and pens or pencils, then give students a few minutes to complete the handout. Make it clear that maybe their greatest need isn't for physical healing, but for the healing of a relationship or the healing of an emotional hurt.

When most have finished, ask them to form groups of three or four to share what they've written. Close in prayer, asking God to help give us more faith in what He can do in us, through us and around us.

Option 2: In Need of Healing. You need blank paper and pens or pencils.

Explain that the bleeding woman in Mark 5 had gone to many doctors and spent all of her money and still did not get better. There is no mention of a support system of friends that came with her to seek Christ. Maybe more people would come to Christ if they had a Christian friend that would love them through a difficult time.

Distribute the paper and pens or pencils and then invite students to write the names of five people in their lives that need healing—not just physical healing, but the healing of a relationship or the healing of an emotional hurt or the spiritual healing that can come through a relationship with God.

When they have done so, encourage them to call, email or write a note to encourage them, and then pray for them every day this week, trusting that God can heal them.

HELP MY UNBELIEF

I can relate to the dad's prayer in Mark 9:24, "I do believe: Help me overcome my unbelief" in the following ways:

I have faith that God is . . .

_____

_____

_____

I have faith that God can . . .

_____

_____

_____

One area in my life I have a need for healing (physical, emotional or relational) is . . .

_____

_____

_____

_____

Rate the following statement on a scale from 0 to 10 (0 indicating no faith and 10 indicating a lot of faith):

The amount of faith I have that Jesus will heal that area is . . .

0   1   2   3   4   5   6   7   8   9   10

God, given the amount of faith I have circled above, help me . . .

_____

_____

_____

_____

One thing I can do this week that might increase my faith is . . .

_____

_____

_____

_____

_____

REFLECT

The following short devotions are for the students to reflect on and answer during the week. You can make a copy of these pages and distribute to your class or print out from the PDF for this session found on *The Life of Jesus* DVD.

1—FAITH FOR HEALING

Jump up and flip to Acts 14:8-10!

Jessie has had a cough for a few weeks. She's gone to the doctor but the doctor said there was nothing she could do to make the cough go away. It was waking Jessie up in the middle of the night and making her feel miserable.

One night, she was sitting in church when the pastor asked if anyone needed prayer for healing. Jessie raised her hand. *After all,* she thought, *if God can't help me, who can?*

Having faith that God will heal you is sometimes a big part of getting well. Do you have faith that God can heal you? Pray that God will help your faith to increase and that you will trust Him more.

2—ASKING RIGHT

Try to look up James 5:13-15 while holding your Bible upside down.

Imagine you are the best omelet maker in the world. How would you feel if two people came to you and asked you for an omelet in the following ways?

- "Hey, um, everyone says you made great omelets, but I'm not sure I believe it. Why don't you make me one and prove it?"

- "Hi, Omelet Maker. Would you make me an awesome omelet? I know you will make me a great one. Thanks."

Sometimes people ask God for healing because they want Him to prove that He can do it. How do you think God wants to be asked?

_____

_____

_____

_____

_____

Do you think God wants you to ask Him to prove what He can do or to simply ask Him and trust that He will do it? Explain.

_____

_____

_____

_____

_____

_____

3—THINGS UNSEEN

Hurry over to Hebrews 11:1!

Neil's sister was making bread. She put flour, water, yeast and a dash of sugar together and made some dough. She put the dough into a bowl, covered the bowl with a dishtowel and left it to rise.

Neil was very skeptical and told his sister, "That lump of goo will never become a loaf of bread no matter what you do to it! Look at it, it doesn't look anything like bread!"

When Neil was asked to have a little faith, he said "Faith?! I gotta see something before I can have any faith!"

Some people have a mixed-up idea of what faith is. God tells us that faith is when you put your trust in something that can't be seen with your eyes, heard with your ears or felt with your hands. Ask God to help you have more faith today.

4—MOVING MOUNTAINS

Thinking of moving mountains? Go to Mark 11:22-26 for a tip.

Imagine that you have five WWF wrestlers who are helping you to move furniture from your house into a moving van. What do you think those big guys could carry?

- Drink coasters and little, pretty knickknacks
- Old magazines (one at a time, of course)
- Pillows and small blankets
- A grand piano, two refrigerators and a pool table

Do you ever ask God to help you with the little things when you've got bigger things that you really need help with? Can you think of a situation in which you've underestimated what God can do for you?

_____

_____

_____

_____

_____

Ask God to help you with one of those big things that you are facing right now, and have faith that He will do it!

DO YOU WANT IT?

THE BIG IDEA

Sometimes you must truly desire help and healing before you can receive them.

SESSION AIMS

In this session you will guide students to (1) understand the reasons people often don't ask for help; (2) be motivated to ask for help to meet their own needs, even if they have something to lose by doing it; and (3) figure out how they can ask for help from God and others.

THE BIGGEST VERSE

"When Jesus saw him lying there and learned that he had been in this condition for a long time, he asked him, 'Do you want to get well?'" (John 5:6).

OTHER IMPORTANT VERSES

Proverbs 27:17; Matthew 9:2,29; 15:28; 22:37-40; Mark 1:31,34; 2:5; 10:52; Luke 13:11-13; 14:4; 22:51; John 5:1-15; 2 Corinthians 1:3-7; Ephesians 4:15

STARTER

Option 1: White Elephant. You need three wrapped prizes: two really cool ones and one that's a little unusual or undesirable—a white-elephant gift.

Greet students and let them know that you're going to play a quick scavenger hunt game with a twist. You're going to name an item and the first student to find the item *on his or her person* and stand up wins that round. Ask for each of these items one at a time: a paper clip, a school ID card and a ticket stub. (If no one has any of these, name some other items such as a penny, a comb, a shoestring, and so forth—anything that you think at least one person might have.) Have the three winners come forward for their prizes.

Starting with the student who had the paper clip, have him or her pick one of the gifts and open it. The student who had the school ID may now pick either of the two remaining wrapped gifts or take the first winner's gift. If Winner Two chooses to take Winner One's gift, Winner One gets to choose one of the remaining wrapped gifts. Either way, the second gift must be opened.

Winner Three may now choose between the last wrapped gift or one of the other winners' gifts. If Winner Three takes one of the other winners' gifts, the person left without a gift now gets to unwrap the last one. Whew! Got it?

Ask the student who got stuck with the white-elephant prize:

- How do you feel about your gift compared to the other two?
- Did it occur to you while you were comparing what you got to the other gifts that the rest of the group didn't get anything at all?

Explain that it's easy to look at all the things that others have and feel sorry for ourselves, focusing on what we don't have. Sometimes life gives us a bum deal, especially if we have difficult challenges or illnesses. Today, we're going to see how Jesus would respond to us when we're feeling sorry for ourselves or about our situations. You might be surprised by what He would have to say!

Option 2: Grateful Relay. You need several packages of individually wrapped LifeSaver candies and several willing-to-look-in-a-junior-higher's-mouth adult leaders! *EWW!*

Greet students and divide them into teams of six. Instruct teams to form lines facing the front of the room. Give each student five unwrapped LifeSaver candies and tell them not to eat them yet! Explain the rules: When you give the signal, the first team member in each line will eat all of his or her candy. After they have eaten all of their candy, they will raise their hands to signal a judge to examine their mouths. If there's no candy left in their mouths, the judge will whisper a letter of the alphabet to each person, and they have to name three things he or she is grateful for. After the first person has named three things, he or she will move to the back of the line and the next person in line will have his or her turn. Team members caught eating their candy before their turn will cost their team a five-second penalty! The first team to finish wins the rest of the candy.

After awarding the prize to the winning team, discuss the following:

- On a scale of 1 to 10, 1 being super easy and 10 being super tough, how hard was it to think of three things you were grateful for?

- What do you spend more time thinking about: things you *don't* have but wish you did or things you *do* have?

- What does that say about your attitude?

- What are the advantages of focusing on what we don't have that we wish we did?

- What are the costs to us?

Suggest that sometimes it's easier to think about all the things we want than to focus on what we have. Sometimes life gives us a bum deal, especially if we have difficult challenges or illnesses. Today you're going to see how Jesus would respond to us when we're feeling sorry for ourselves or for our situations. You might be surprised by what He would say!

MESSAGE

Option 1: Inner Tube Tug-of-War. You need an open area, a large inflated inner tube and masking tape. Ahead of time, use the tape to mark two long parallel lines approximately 20 feet apart; then mark another smaller line down the middle between the first two.

At the meeting, select an equal number of students and volunteers for the game and designate the remaining students as the cheering section. (*Note*: This tug-of-war works best with students wearing sturdy shoes and modest attire—no dresses!) Place half of the contestants along one of the lines and half on the other, making sure to match strength/size on both teams *in the same order.* (In other words, don't line up the smallest person on Team A across from an adult leader on Team B.) Assign each team member a number, making sure that his or her matched opponent on the other side has the same number, and then place the inner tube on the smaller line in the middle of the area.

Explain the game: You'll call out a random number and the player on each team who has that number must try to grab the inner tube and bring it over to his or her team's side. If both opponents get their hands on the tube and a tug-of-war results for longer than 10 seconds, you will yell out "Helpers!" and each opponent can call out the name of one person on his or her team to run out and help. The team that successfully gets the inner tube into its area wins that round.

Play several rounds (it can be fun to call out several numbers for the last one) and the team that gets the inner tube into its area the most times wins the game. After everyone catches his or her breath, discuss the following:

- Was it nice to know that your team was ready and waiting to help if you needed it?

- Was it easier to play the game when you had someone from your team to help you?

- Thinking about your life in general, when is it easiest for you to ask for help?

- When is it hardest?

Distribute Bibles and read John 5:1-15 aloud.[1] Explain that after being confined to a bed for 38 years, obviously the crippled man would be so weak that he probably couldn't even stand on his own. He might have been one of the neediest people around the pool—and maybe that's why Jesus selected him.

Ask the students why they think Jesus would ask the man if he wanted to be healed (see v. 6). (He may have been interested in whether the man would

Youth Leader Tip

Games are more than just a fun way to fill the time—they are also a way to bring teens together to share laughter and life. When your students experience enjoyable times together, they will be ready to study the Word and participate in the church to a greater extent.[2]

be willing to give up the income he could make as a crippled beggar; maybe He was using the question to see how much will and desire the man had to be healed.) Suggest that there are often two reasons we don't ask for help: (1) We have tried and it hasn't worked; or (2) we're actually not sure if we want to be free from the position we're in.

Option 2: Helping the Helpless. You need Bibles and one set of the following items for every four students: a magazine, several pieces of unlined paper, a pen or pencil, a glue stick and a pair of scissors.

Divide students into groups of four and distribute a set of the listed items to each group. Instruct the groups to look through the magazines to cut out a picture of someone who needs help. If they can't find someone in obvious need, they should be creative and diagnose a need for someone. Instruct the groups to glue the pictures to their papers and place the diagnosed need as a caption underneath the picture. On the back of the paper, they should write all the ways that the person could be helped. Allow several minutes for groups to create their profiles, then invite representatives from each group to share their results.

Have students read John 5:1-15 using the popcorn method, in which students read a verse and then call the name of another student to continue with another verse, until the passage is done. Discuss:

1. What does the saying, "You can lead a horse to water, but you can't make him drink" mean? *You can give someone everything he or she needs, but you can't make him or her use it.*

2. How does that saying fit into this passage? *The man was at the pool every day, but he couldn't (or didn't) get into the water to be healed.*

3. How might the saying describe the people in the picture projects you did?

4. Could the person in your picture be helped if he or she didn't want to be?

5. How would you describe the man's attitude before Jesus healed him? *He had a pessimistic attitude, an I-can't-because-of-my-circumstances attitude.*

6. What was he focused on? *He was focused on his limitations.*

7. What was the man's attitude after Jesus healed him? *He obeyed
    and walked away. It doesn't say so, but he was probably very happy.*

Explain that there were two reasons the crippled man might not have
wanted help: (1) He benefited from his problem because people gave him
money, or (2) he didn't think anyone would help him. How might these reasons relate to the pictures the student groups chose?

DIG

Option 1: A Little Help from My Friends. To do this option, you just need this
here book. Begin by reading the following case study:

Ramon is a student leader in his youth group. As a junior in high school,
there are many younger students that look to him for an example of a
Christian. He's an athlete, active in many things at school and has a
steady girlfriend.

Ramon and his girlfriend, Nadia, have been dating for over a year
and both feel that their relationship will last a long time—maybe even
ending in marriage way down the road. Ramon loves Nadia and feels
that sex would take their relationship to a new level, but he also knows
what the Bible says about premarital sex. He's counseled other students
and advised them to wait. He even made a commitment at a purity
seminar to wait until he's married to engage in sexual activity, but he's
having doubts about his own willpower.

Ramon knows he should call a Christian friend or his youth pastor
to help sort out all the issues, but if he does, they'll know how weak he
really is, and worse, they'll know he's a hypocrite. He's not even sure he
wants to hear what they have to say because he really thinks he and his
girlfriend would benefit from this new level of intimacy.

Next, discuss the following:

1. What would you do if you were Ramon?

2. How much does he want help? *He's probably torn between the temp-
    tation of wanting something and needing help to keep from doing it.*

3. What would he do if he really wanted help to do the right thing? *He would find someone to help him understand what is the right thing to do and challenge him to do the right thing.*

4. How could he ask Jesus to help him? *By prayer and Bible study.*

5. How could he ask others to help him? *He could ask an adult to be his spiritual mentor or a Christian friend to keep him accountable— someone to pray with him and to ask him if he is keeping pure.*

Option 2: Help—Who Needs It? You need the following questions to lead an in-depth discussion:

1. Assuming that the crippled man did not have faith, why did Jesus make him well? *God often does wonderful things for those who don't know Him—for reasons sometimes only He understands. He may bless someone's business, heal a disease or help out a family, simply out of His love for all mankind and His desire to see every one of His children come to a saving knowledge of Jesus Christ. It's the ultimate statement of His grace and mercy that He blesses people even when they don't give Him credit.*

2. In John 5:14, Jesus told the man to stop sinning or something worse could happen. What's worse than being crippled for 38 years? *Humans sin—we all make mistakes that can cost us a lot. Jesus was warning the man to avoid the biggest cost of all: eternal separation from God. Out of love, Jesus warned the man to turn to God and away from his sin because the man really needed spiritual healing even more than physical healing.*

3. Is it possible to survive without ever asking for help from anyone? *Technically, yes, but it would be a pretty exhausting life. You would have to find and/or kill all of your own food, prepare it, clean up, find a place to live, make your own clothes—you get the idea. Just plain exhausting. It might be possible, but why would anyone want to?*

APPLY

Option 1: Got Help? You need enough copies of "Got Help?" (found on the next page and on *The Life of Jesus* DVD) for everyone, and pens or pencils.

got help?

One problem I have is . . .

_____
_____
_____
_____

This problem makes me feel . . .

_____
_____
_____
_____

If I were to ask God for help, I'd probably ask Him to . . .
    (Write down as many things as you can think of.)

_____
_____
_____
_____
_____

Some ways other people could help me are . . .
    (Write down as many things as you can think of.)

_____
_____
_____
_____
_____

Some things I could do to get help from God or others are . . .

_____
_____
_____
_____
_____

Point out that there's not a single person here who doesn't have some problem in his or her life. Maybe they haven't asked God for help because they think He doesn't really care or because He's too distant or because He doesn't have time for them or one of a million other reasons. Maybe they haven't asked others for help because they don't think they care or because they're too busy or because they've asked before and others haven't helped at all.

Distribute "Got Help?" and pens or pencils and allow five minutes for students to complete the handout. Ask them to circle any of their answers to the last question that they're willing to try this week. Invite a few of them to share what they've circled.

Close in prayer, thanking God for His desire to help us even with the least of our problems and asking Him to help students to learn to bring all of their problems and concerns to Him.

Option 2: Helping Others. You need several Bibles, a whiteboard and a dry-erase marker.

Point out that there's one tragic note in the story of the crippled man. Ask the group if anyone can see what it is. Give them the following hints, one at a time: It involves a man who was healed. It involves other people still left at the pool. It involves what the man could have done for them. The answer is simple: *The once crippled, now perfectly healthy man, could have gone back and helped other people into the pool.*

Explain that we are often like that man: Jesus helps us with something and then we move on, selfishly ignoring the needs of others around us. Distribute the Bibles and ask for a volunteer to read 2 Corinthians 1:3-7. Discuss:

1. What things has Jesus helped you with in the last month? (Allow students to suggest a few incidents such as help with a test, help with handling anger or wisdom about how to handle a tricky friendship situation. The sky is the limit—and so is God's helping hand!)

Youth Leader Tip

Be sure to look for ways to work with other youth workers in your area. Combined events make for less work, and when students see you building relationships with leaders of other churches, they will be more likely to hang out with believers from those churches.

2. How can remembering how Jesus helps us make a difference in the way we help others? *We might be more willing to help others if we remind ourselves how He has helped us.*

Close in prayer, giving students a chance to thank God for ways He has helped them and to ask Him to show them ways to comfort and help others.

REFLECT

The following short devotions are for the students to reflect on and answer during the week. You can make a copy of these pages and distribute to your class or print out from the PDF for this session found on *The Life of Jesus* DVD.

1—YOU HAVE TO ASK!

Hey! Stop and read Acts 5:12-16 right this second!

Kelly was so mad! Her mom packed her a tuna sandwich *again*, and Kelly was so sick of tuna. Mom didn't pick Kelly up from school, so she had to walk home. Worst of all, Mom didn't wash Kelly's gym clothes, so they smelled sweaty and gross.

As soon as she got home, Kelly told her mom how mad she was at her—and exactly why.

"But, honey," Kelly's mom said, "you didn't tell me you wanted or needed anything. I just assumed everything was all right."

It is true that God knows our every need, but He wants us to ask Him for help. Do you ever try to take care of things yourself, even though you would like God's help?

Ask God to help you with all your needs today.

2—WHAT ARE YOU WAITING FOR?

Go to Luke 5:12-16 and get the scoop!

Imagine you have a problem that you know your friend can fix. Do you . . .

- ❏ Try to fix it yourself, even though you wish your friend was helping you?
- ❏ Look on the Internet for a remedy?
- ❏ Ignore it and hope it goes away?
- ❏ Ask your friend to help you?

God wants to help us solve our problems. When you're sick and need healing, do you ask Him for help? Or do you try to take care of it yourself?

Does your body or heart need healing? Have you asked God to heal you? Try it now—pray and believe that He will help you!

3—WHY SHOULD I PRAY?

This will be on the quiz: Psalm 102:17.

Tim's mom sat him down on the couch in the living room last Thursday and told him that she had been diagnosed with breast cancer. She was scheduled to have surgery right away. Tim was really scared and sad and angry at God. When his best friend, Jake, told Tim to pray for healing, Tim said angrily, "No way! God's mean if He let this happen to my mom. Why should I pray?"

Do you think Tim is right? God does hear us when we pray and He does heal the sick—even though sometimes it's not in a way we can see. When we pray to Him, He is very concerned about what is going on in our lives; and even when miraculous healing doesn't happen, God is still there, loving everyone involved.

Do you need to ask God for healing today? Go ahead, do it now!

4—JUST KNOCK ON THE DOOR!

Knock, knock. Who's there? Matthew 7:7-8!

You need to get into your Aunt Lulu's house. In order to get inside, you . . .

- ❏ Stand outside the door and wait.
- ❏ Try all of your keys to unlock her door (even your locker key!).
- ❏ Sing "The Wheels on the Bus" really loudly.
- ❏ Knock.

Talking to God is as simple as knocking on a door. Do you ever make it more difficult than that? Or do you avoid knocking altogether?

Ask God in a simple way for what you need and thank Him for all He has done for you already.

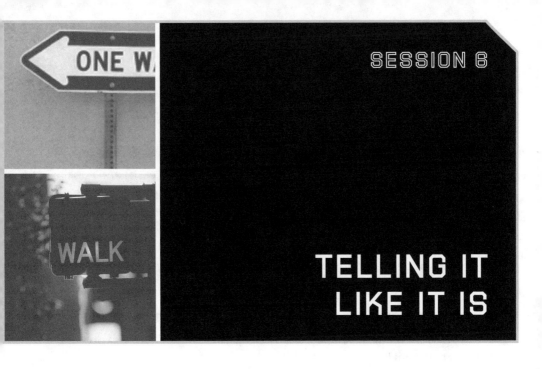

TELLING IT LIKE IT IS

THE BIG IDEA

Telling the story of all God has done in your own life can have a tremendous impact on others.

SESSION AIMS

In this session you will guide students to (1) understand the power of sharing about what Jesus has done in their lives with someone else; (2) experience how grateful someone would be to get his or her sight back; and (3) be empowered to use conversations and their testimonies to reach others.

THE BIGGEST VERSE

"Then they asked him, 'What did he do to you? How did he open your eyes?' He answered, 'I have told you already and you did not listen. Why do you want to hear it again? Do you want to become his disciples, too?'" (John 9:26-27).

OTHER IMPORTANT VERSES

Exodus 20:4-6; Deuteronomy 28:15,21-22; Matthew 5:14-16; John 9:1-39; Acts 6:7; Romans 5:1-5,12; James 4:2; Revelation 21:4

STARTER

Option 1: Art Contest. You need an adult volunteer, paper napkins and enough Starburst candies for each student to have three pieces. *Option*: Bubble gum could be used in place of the candy.

Greet students and distribute the candy (three pieces each) and napkins. At your signal, students are to chew all of their candy at once—but not swallow. They will have one minute to form a "masterpiece" in their mouths without removing the candy or touching it with their fingers. After one minute, signal for students to spit out their candy sculptures onto their napkins. Ask the adult volunteer to judge the sculptures and award the rest of the candy to the winner (the unopened, unchewed pieces, of course!). Discuss:

- Was it difficult not being able to see what you were creating?
- Why would it have been easier to see your masterpiece as you were creating it?
- How important is your vision in everyday life?
- What would you miss the most if you couldn't see?
- Are there any advantages to not having your sight?
- If you had been blind and your sight was suddenly restored, what would be the first thing you would want to do?

Explain that today you're going to study someone who got his sight back in a miraculous way. He was grateful, of course, but you might be surprised at some of the things he did first.

Option 2: Blind for a Morning. You need four blindfolds, four chairs, a baggy, button-front shirt and pants, a hairbrush, some makeup, a table and chair, milk, cereal, a bowl and a spoon. Ahead of time, set the four chairs up in front of the room facing the audience.

Youth Leader Tip

As often as you can, take pictures of your students. Photos can help volunteers get to know students, can be added to flyers and other mailers, and they can be used in various audiovisual presentations (junior-highers love to see their faces on screen!).

At the meeting, welcome students and ask for four volunteers. Give the shirt and pants to the first volunteer, the hairbrush to the second, the makeup to the third and seat the fourth at the table with the milk, cereal, bowl and spoon. Blindfold the volunteers and ask them to do these fairly routine morning exercises:

Volunteer One: Put on the shirt and pants.
Volunteer Two: Brush your hair.
Volunteer Three: Apply the makeup.
Volunteer Four: Pour the cereal and milk and eat breakfast.

Allow a few minutes for the volunteers to attempt the tasks, and then applaud their efforts and invite them to return to their seats. Discuss the following with the whole group:

- Do you know anybody who is blind?

- How do you feel when you see someone who is blind?

- How do you think you would feel if you were blind?

- Which would be easier: becoming blind as a junior-higher or being born blind?

- Are there any advantages to not having your sight?

- If you had been born blind and your sight were suddenly restored, what would you want to do first?

Explain that today you're going to study someone who got his sight back in a miraculous way. He was grateful, of course, but you might be surprised at some of the things he did first.

MESSAGE

Option 1: Acting Up. You need several Bibles, one copy of "Acting Up" (found on the next page and on *The Life of Jesus* DVD) and candy for prizes.

Ahead of time, cut the individual statements on the handout into 10 individual slips of paper.

Divide students into teams—ideally, 8 to 15 students per team. Distribute Bibles and explain that students are going to act out the Bible story from John

ACTING UP

1. The Jews still did not believe that He had been blind and had received his sight" (John 9:18).

2. "A man blind from birth" (John 9:1).

3. "He spit on the ground, made some mud with the saliva" (John 9:6).

4. "A second time they summoned the man who had been blind" (John 9:24).

5. " 'Where is this man?' they asked Him" (John 9:12).

6. "I was blind but now I see" (John 9:25).

7. "He is a prophet" (John 9:17).

8. "Do you want to become his disciples, too?" (John 9:27).

9. "The Jews had decided that anyone who acknowledged that Jesus was the Christ would be put out of the synagogue" (John 9:22).

10. "So the man went and washed, and came home seeing" (John 9:7).

9:1-39 in stages. Give them a moment to read through the story in their groups. Then one at a time, teams will send up one person. This student will be given one of the 10 verses *at random* to act out using only body language— no words. As the student acts out the verse, the teams will compete to match his or her actions to a verse found in John 9:1-39. The team that correctly identifies the verse by standing up and reading it earns 2,000 points.

Play until all 10 verses have been identified; then tally the points and award candy prizes to the winning team. Ask students which verse stood out the most to them.

Next, ask volunteers to read Deuteronomy 28:15,21-22, the results of disobeying God, and Exodus 20:4-6, the second of the Ten Commandments. Now reread John 9:1-2 and explain it using the following information:

> The Old Testament clearly teaches (1) that sin can lead to sickness (see Deuteronomy 28:15,21-22) and (2) that sin and the punishment for sin (which can include sickness) can move from generation to generation of those who "hate" (reject) God (see Exodus 20:4-5).
>
> When the disciples asked, "Who sinned, this man, or his parents?" they were not asking, "Why do the innocent suffer?" They were assuming, based on what they had read in the Old Testament, that sin could lead to sickness.
>
> Notice that in His response, Jesus did not reject the Old Testament idea that personal sin or the sins of one's parents or grandparents could cause sickness. Rather, He rejected the idea that sin or the parents' or grandparents' sin was the cause of blindness in this particular case. Jesus gave the disciples an explanation that they were completely unprepared for: that in this case, the purpose of the man's blindness was to bring glory to God.
>
> This really upset the Pharisees in the story, because not only was Jesus healing on the Sabbath (and thus breaking their interpretation of the fourth commandment), but He also had healed someone who, in their view, deserved blindness because he was "steeped in sin at birth" (John 9:34).

Before he was through, the man who had been healed of blindness called Jesus "a prophet" (v. 17), "from God" (v. 33), the "Son of Man" (vv. 35-36) and actually concluded by worshiping Jesus as "Lord" (v. 38). The man had progressed from darkness into light, both physically and spiritually.

Option 2: Washing Up. You need several Bibles, a large bucket, water, dirt, candy and a blank personal check. Ahead of time, mix the water and dirt together in the bucket to make mud.

Ask for volunteers who like the feel of mud, explaining that it's an important part of the story. (You're probably more likely to get guys to come forward, and that's okay.) Invite the volunteers to stick their hands in the mud, then instruct them to go wash their hands. The catch? You're going to convince them that they need to go to some out-of-the-way sink, water fountain or outside spigot, somewhere farther than where they might typically go to wash their hands. Fabricate some reason they need to go farther, such as they'll make too much noise and disturb another class.

When the volunteers return from washing their hands, take a quick survey of who followed your directions and went to the farthest place to wash up. Reward those who went the farthest with candy, then explain that this lesson ties into Jesus' miracle recorded in John 9:1-39. Read the passage aloud then explain that in this story we see three things that faith causes us to do:

1. *It causes us to act.* The man didn't know what the mud was going to do, nor did he know why Jesus wanted him to go to the Pool of Siloam, which was probably not the closest water source. His faith caused him to act and do what Jesus wanted him to do. The same is true with the students who went the farthest to wash their hands—they had faith that you were telling them the right thing to do.

2. *It causes us to be blessed.* The man got a tangible reward: healing. Those who went the farthest to wash up also got a tangible reward: candy. Sometimes our blessings aren't that tangible—they're more intangibles (such as peace, joy, more faith, a sense of hope) that we wouldn't have without our faith in Jesus. These may not be tangible, but they are eternal through Him!

3. *It causes us to talk.* Write a check to one of your students for a million dollars. Yes, a million dollars! Ask that student: If you knew how to get a million dollars for yourself and everyone else you know, would you tell everyone? Of course they would. But they have an awesome opportunity to have something even more valuable: a priceless relationship with Jesus Christ. The man in this story knew

this and told others about how Jesus had changed his life. (Okay, okay . . . void the check now, just in case you're one of those super rich youth workers we've heard so much about and your check could actually be cashed!)

DIG

Option 1: A Good Story. For this option, you need just this story. Read the following case study to the whole group:

Matthew has gone to church all his life. Ever since he was old enough to be left in the nursery, he has been taught the stories of Noah, Daniel and the lion's den, and David and Goliath. He accepted Jesus as his Savior at an early age and wants to serve Him.

Since Matthew got into junior high, though, he's become increasingly aware that his testimony isn't very exciting. His friend, Elizabeth, has a dramatic story of how Jesus saved her from a difficult life. Matthew knows he has a good family and that he's never really done anything horrible, but he feels a little inferior to those whose lives were drastically changed by the Savior.

Matthew knows that there are a lot of people at his school that need the love of Jesus in their lives. He wants to reach them, but he also feels that a boring story about a church boy isn't going to motivate many people to come to Christ. He has resolved himself to make up a story of drug use, physical abuse and deceit to make his story more exciting. He knows lying is wrong, but he is trying to do what he thinks is best for serving Christ.

Ask students what they think Matthew should do. After they come up with some ideas, ask if it is ever a good idea to lie in order to help someone become

Youth Leader Tip

Relationships are the key to effective youth ministry. The greatest programs will fail and the most interesting curriculum will never be absorbed by students if your primary focus is not on building solid, encouraging, positive relationships with them.[1]

a Christian. (Absolutely not! There are many reasons, but this one is a must-know: God is truth. His message does not need to be distorted to be believed—and whatever He does in any individual, whether boring in our view or not, is worthy of praise; it doesn't need to be exaggerated!)

Option 1: The Five Ws. You need copies of "The Five Ws . . ." (found on the next page and on *The Life of Jesus* DVD) for everyone, and pens or pencils.

Distribute "The Five Ws" and pens or pencils. Invite students to take a few minutes to think about what they might say if someone asked them when, where, why and how they became a Christian. Allow a few minutes to complete the handout, and then divide students into groups of three to share their answers with each other. *Note:* Suggest that students who haven't yet asked Jesus to be their Savior and take over their lives answer the handout questions by applying them to when they started coming to church.

Explain to the group that these papers signify their personal testimony for Jesus, just like the testimony given by the blind man. They don't have to be a pastor or youth leader to have a story and they don't have to know all the answers. All they need to share is how knowing Jesus has changed them, and only they know that!

APPLY

Option 1: Be a Light. You need a flashlight for this option.

Explain that Jesus said, "While I am in the world, I am the light of the world" (John 9:5). In Matthew 5:14-16, He tells us that *we* are "the light of the world." While fellowship with our Christian friends is a necessity for support, it's also important to share Christ with non-Christians in our lives, just as the formerly blind man did after Jesus healed him. Jesus in us is the light that others need to see.

Place the flashlight in the middle of the room (turned off) and dim the lights. Invite students who are willing to be a light for Jesus to come forward one at a time, pick up the flashlight, turn it on and say the name of someone they would like to be a light for and to share Jesus with. *Note:* It's better to have one sincere person come forward than a group of students who are doing it just because everyone else is. Stress the point that only students who are really willing to make a commitment to be a light for others should come forward.

Close in prayer, thanking Jesus for allowing us to be lights in the darkness and asking Him to help each student make a commitment to be a light for Him.

The Five Ws...

*W*here were you when you asked Jesus to take over your life and be your Savior?

_____
_____
_____
_____
_____

*W*ho were you with?

_____
_____
_____
_____
_____

*W*hat do you remember about it?

_____
_____
_____
_____
_____

*W*hy did you do it?

_____
_____
_____
_____
_____

*W*hen and *how* has it made a difference in your life?

_____
_____
_____
_____
_____

Option 2: Table Talk. For this option, you will need plastic forks, knives, spoons, cups and napkins.

Explain that we never know when we might have a chance to explain to someone how and why we became a Christian. Telling our own story is really important, but it's also a good idea to know God's story: the reasons why He sent Jesus and what Jesus did for us.

Distribute the plastic forks, knives, spoons, cups and napkins, and then ask the students to imagine that they are at a restaurant getting some food with some friends and someone asks why they go to church. The student tells them that it's because they like to learn about God, at which point one of their Mormon friends says, "Yeah, me too. I guess our churches are pretty much the same, right?" This is probably a pretty good chance to explain some basic Christian beliefs!

At this point, have students pair off and take turns explaining the basics of Christianity to each other. You can walk them through it, using the cups and utensils to illustrate: The cup is God. The spoon and fork represent people, but we're a long way from God because sin separates us from Him (place the cup several inches away from the spoon and fork; then place the napkin between the cup and the tableware). That's why God sent Jesus (the knife) as a bridge between us and God (place the knife on top of the napkin). Now we can ask Jesus to take over our lives, be our Savior and Lord and help us walk back across to God.

Practice this several times and ask for a few students to demonstrate in front of the whole group if you have time. Close in prayer, thanking God for opportunities every day to share His light with people and asking Him to give students courage to share their own stories—and His.

Youth Leader Tip

Remember that with junior-highers, the more visual, the better. They'll remember the objects you used in a talk long after they've forgotten everything else you said. It will also help them when they are attempting to explain the gospel message to others that they know.

REFLECT

The following short devotions are for the students to reflect on and answer during the week. You can make a copy of these pages and distribute to your class or print out from the PDF for this session found on *The Life of Jesus* DVD.

1—BETTER THAN A UNICYCLE

Listen up and flip to Romans 10:16-17.

Imagine that you own a unicycle and you really love it. Your friend has seen you riding it and he's thinking about getting one for himself. What would you tell him about it?

- ❒ "Um, it's cool. Yeah, it's cool."
- ❒ "I fall off of it all the time—you'd hate it."
- ❒ "It's cool for me, but you'd probably think it's dumb."
- ❒ "It's a lot of hard work but it's so much fun. If you get one, I'll teach you how to ride it. Okay?"

Believe it or not, people want to hear what your relationship with God is like! Do you tell people the things He has done for you? Or do you keep it all inside like a secret?

Who is one person you can talk to today about all that Jesus has done for you? How will you tell him or her?

_____

_____

_____

_____

2—GO TELL IT

Read Hebrews 13:15-16 and don't forget it!

Paul had known Jesus for a few years and he really loved Him a lot. Even though he didn't always get it right, his relationship with God was really important to him. He studied his Bible, prayed and worked in the nursery at his church on Sunday mornings.

Sometimes he really wanted to tell his friends about how Jesus was the best thing that had ever happened to him, but he was scared. *After all,* he reasoned, *I don't have a cool story like God's saving me from a pouncing cheetah or anything like that. Why would they care?*

Telling others about what God has done in your life is a fantastic thing to do! You may not think that your story is very cool, but other people need to hear what God has done for you.

Pray that God will give you the courage to share that with at least one person today.

3—I'M SO EXCITED

Are you excited? Go to Romans 12:11-13 to see why you should be!

So how can you tell when someone you know is really excited and happy about something?

- ❏ They hold their head in their hands and moan, "Oh, no!"
- ❏ They sit very quietly, humming and twiddling their thumbs.
- ❏ They talk about other things, like their ingrown toenail.
- ❏ They run around telling everyone they see about it.

God wants us to be really excited about our relationship with Him, just as He is excited about His relationship with you. Do you act like you're excited when you tell other people about Jesus?

What are some ways you can be more excited about everything that Jesus has done for you?

_____

_____

_____

_____

4—CAN YOU HEAR ME NOW?

Be a shiny, happy person by reading Matthew 5:16!

Everyone knew Karina was in love with Jesus. She told everyone how happy He made her—her teachers, her parents, her brother and sister, the mailman, the pizza guy and people on the street. It didn't even matter where she was—she talked to people at the movies, in fast-food restaurants and at school . . . even during gym! Karina just couldn't shut up about how much she loved God and how she wanted others to get to know Him, too!

Does talking about God make you excited? Or is it something you would rather not do?

It's scary at first, but people really do want to hear what you have to say, especially when you're really excited about it.

Write the names of the people you want to tell how cool Jesus is and put the list where you will see it every day.

_____

_____

_____

_____

HOW TO WORSHIP GOD

EVEN WHEN YOU'RE NOT SINGING

Worship. What does the word mean to you? A boring church service? A bunch of people wearing choir robes and singing? Well, get this: Your whole life can be worship!

In Romans 12:1, Paul gives us a biblical definition of worship: "Therefore, I urge you, brothers, in view of God's mercy, to offer your bodies as living sacrifices, holy and pleasing to God—this is your spiritual act of worship." The good news here is that Paul doesn't mean sacrifices to be killed, but rather *living* sacrifices. Your life and body belong to God. God wants you to live a holy life that pleases Him. That's worship!

In Colossians 3:17, Paul gives us another measure for worship: "And whatever you do, whether in word or deed, do it all in the name of the Lord Jesus, giving thanks to God the Father through him." *Whatever* you say, *whatever* you do, all of it can be worship if you do it in Jesus' name, giving thanks to God. So where should you start? Here are a few ideas:

Worship God Through Sharing His Love

Jesus came to die for the world. He wants everyone to know about His amazing love for us. As John writes in 1 John 4:7, "Dear friends, let us love one another, for love comes from God." You show your intense love for Jesus as you introduce your friends to Him.

Worship God Through Strengthening Your Relationship

Jesus wants you to love Him with all your heart, soul and mind (see Matthew 22:37). It will be easier to do that when you read your Bible and other books that focus your mind on Him. Pray. Take a walk with Him. Try making a list of everything He's given you to be thankful for. Sit and be quiet. Get to know your Best Friend.

Worship God Through Your Friendships

"A man of many companions may come to ruin," says Proverbs 18:24, "but there is a friend who sticks closer than a brother." Worship God by choosing your friends wisely—and then be wise about the ways that you spend time together. Your friends will either help or hurt you in your relationship with God. If they help you, worship will come more easily. If not, you're better off with other friends.

Worship God Through Service

In Ephesians 6:7, Paul urges us to "serve wholeheartedly, as if you were serving the Lord, not men." Worship God by doing some extra chores around the house. (Yeah, even volunteer for them!) Mow a neighbor's lawn or take out her trash. Volunteer in the church office. If your school has a service club, join. If there isn't one, start one. Once you start looking for opportunities to serve, you'll see them everywhere.

Worship God Through Celebration

Jesus came to bring you an abundant, joyful life (see John 10:10; 15:11). You worship God when you go to church and celebrate Him with other believers. Yes, sing! Celebrate God's gift of life with extravagant birthday parties. Do something you've always wanted to do. Be who God made you to be: If you're an artist, create; if you're an athlete, play. Take a risk. Love deeply and enjoy life. Involve God in everything you do and everything you do will be an offering of worship.

UNIT II

The Parables of Jesus

This next unit is devoted to helping you and your junior-highers grow in and grasp the stories of Christ. Because most of Jesus' stories were parables, we decided to focus this section on parables as well (after all, if Jesus did it, why shouldn't we?). First, here are a few simple questions that are geared to helping you maximize the impact this unit will have on your students.

Why should we teach junior-highers about Jesus' parables? The main reason to teach junior-highers the stories, especially the parables of Jesus, is that Jesus taught them.

More specifically, parables by their very definition give us three reasons to teach them to junior-highers. First, parables are short and simple stories designed to communicate a spiritual truth or religious principle by illustrating truth through a comparison or example drawn from everyday experiences. Jesus taught with stories because they are often the easiest way to teach eternal truths. This is especially true when you're staring at a roomful of concrete-thinking 13-year-olds.

Second, parables are based on the experiences of the listeners. When Jesus taught almost 2,000 years ago, even the simplest and least educated of listeners could follow His stories because they understood the types of people, the circumstances and the decisions involved.

Finally, parables have one central point. Although many applications could be drawn from Jesus' stories, there was always one major point. This simplicity fits junior-highers perfectly. Their growing minds can only grab on to one or two principles at a time—as you've no doubt experienced when you've tried to teach them more than that!

How should we teach junior-highers about Jesus' parables? As you set out to teach the parables, it is vital that you do two things. First, study the true biblical meaning and depend entirely on God's Word itself. As we learn in Hebrews 4:12, "For the word of God is living and active. Sharper than any doubled-edged sword, it penetrates even to dividing soul and spirit, joints and marrow; it judges the thoughts and attitudes of the heart." Make sure you focus more on what the Bible teaches than on your own common sense.

Second, let the words sink deep into you. Because the parables are eternal truths that are taught through practical everyday stories, you as the teacher must experience these truths yourself. Live their meanings. Only then can you fully understand their lessons. Be a visual aid for your students—and a life-sized one at that!

Miles McPherson
President of Miles Ahead
Senior Pastor of The Rock Church
in San Diego, California

LISTENING TO GOD

THE BIG IDEA

God wants to talk to us. The question is, *Are we ready to listen to Him?*

SESSION AIMS

In this session you will guide students to (1) identify obstacles that make them deaf to what God is trying to say to them; (2) feel comforted knowing that God is actively pursuing them and longs to speak to them; and (3) act by choosing one way they can listen to God this week.

THE BIGGEST VERSE

"He who has ears, let him hear" (Matthew 13:9).

OTHER IMPORTANT VERSES

Psalms 15:1-5; 119:97-104; Matthew 13:1-23

STARTER

Option 1: Have a Ball. For this option, you will need a small ball, a candy prize, paper and pens or pencils.

Greet students and explain that you're starting a new series on the teachings of Jesus, but first you want to do a quick activity together. Explain that you're going to ask a question, then throw the ball to a student. The person who gets the ball should answer the question, then throw the ball to another student, who then answers the same question and throws the ball (and so on). This continues until everyone has answered the question or until you feel momentum is dying and it's time to introduce another question.

Suggested questions include: What is your middle name? What is the third digit in your telephone number? What is the best after-school snack that you have had this week? What is something you can share with us that probably no one else here knows?

After a few minutes, distribute papers and pens or pencils and ask each student to list as many people's answers as they can, such as "José's best after-school snack was eggplant." (José's got some unusual tastes, obviously.)

Give a candy prize to the student who can remember the most answers, and then ask the following questions:

- What made it tough to remember what people said?
- When we're talking with our friends, why is it sometimes hard to listen to them? (Answers may include that we're too busy, distracted and self-centered.)
- Why is it important to listen to the people you care about?
- Why is it important to listen to God?

Suggest that listening is essential for developing a good friendship, whether it is our friendship with God or our friendships with our friends or family. For any friendship to grow stronger, we've got to be willing to listen.

Option 2: Let's Get Talking! You need several sheets of paper and pens or pencils. Divide students into groups of six. Distribute paper and pens or pencils and instruct students to write messages that they might want to communicate to people. Some ideas include phrases like "Hey, I think you're cool!" "You have something caught in your teeth" or "I like that shirt you're wearing today." Allow two minutes for students to write as many statements as they can think of—a different statement on each sheet of paper. When time is up, ask students if they've ever noticed that hearing and understanding what people say isn't always easy. Well, today they're going to have a really hard time hearing people.

Have the small groups stand up and designate two students from each group as the "listeners." Instruct these students to form a circle, standing an arm's length apart and facing toward the middle. Assign two more students from each group the role of the "talkers." Have these students kneel in a tight circle in the middle of the listeners' circle, shoulder to shoulder, facing out toward the listeners. Give the talkers the papers with the statements written on them and instruct them to wad the papers into tight paper balls. The remaining students are the "interferers" who will attempt to obstruct the communication between the talkers and the listeners.

The game works like this: The talkers kneel in their circle and toss the paper wads at the listeners. The interferers run around and try to keep the wads from the listeners. Once a listener has caught a wad of paper, the interferers cannot rip it from his or her hands.

As a signal to get the game started, yell: *Let's get talking!* Give students 90 seconds to play; then have students switch roles and repeat the game.

Once you've calmed them down (with the adrenaline of junior-highers it may take a few minutes), have them sit down; then discuss:

1. How is this game like communication with others? *Sometimes things interfere with communication. Sometimes it's hard to hear our friends.*

2. What are some things that can interfere with our communication with others? (Answers may include getting too busy, self-centered or distracted by other things.)

Transition to a deeper level of discussion by asking for students to think of a time when they had difficulty listening to God. Explain to students that good communication, whether it be with God or others, is the result of both talking and listening. Today we're going to learn how we can listen to God better.

MESSAGE

Option 1: Getting Dirty. You need several Bibles, transparent or masking tape, paper and pens or pencils.

Ahead of time, write the following kinds of soil and their corresponding Scripture passages each on a separate sheet of paper: "the path," Matthew

13:3-4; "the rocky soil," Matthew 13:5-6; "the thorny soil," Matthew 13:7; "the good soil," Matthew 13:8.

At the meeting, explain that you're going to study some of the stories Jesus told to teach us how to live as His followers. When Jesus talked to people about things that were hard to understand, He often used stories called *parables*. That way, even though the things He was saying were hard to understand, the people hearing what He had to say would be able to grasp at least part of what He was saying. In today's story, Jesus used an interesting parable to communicate a powerful truth.[1]

Ask for 10 volunteers to help act out the parable in Matthew 13:1-9. Assign students the following roles: "Farmer," "Seeds," four "Soils" (you will need one volunteer for each of the four soil signs you prepared), "Bird," "Sun" and two "Thorns" (two volunteers to be thorns). *Note*: It's okay if some students play more than one role.

Ask the actors to act out their roles with as much dramatic feeling as possible as you slowly read Matthew 13:1-9; then discuss the following:

1. Who does the farmer represent? *God.*

2. What do the seeds represent? *God's Word, the truths that He is trying to show us.*

3. What are the differences between the four types of soil? *They were different in their willingness to receive or hear the truth that God was trying to give them.*

Next, read Jesus' explanation of this parable from Matthew 13:18-23. Continue by asking the following questions:

1. What do you think Jesus wanted His listeners to learn from this parable? *It's important to listen to God and allow Him to change our hearts*

Youth Leader Tip

When you feel that you aren't communicating with your group, try exaggerating everything you are talking about. Shout directions. Stand on your head. Of course, remember that there is a fine line between acting crazy and looking stupid, so find the line and live above it.

to become more like His. We need to prepare the "soil" of our hearts to receive His Word and allow it to grow.

2. What things might be considered rocks or thorns in our lives? *Sin, distractions or being too busy to spend time with God.*

As you close this option, help students understand the importance of removing the things in our lives that keep us from hearing God.

Option 2: Getting the Latest Dirt. You need several Bibles, enough copies of "Getting the Latest Dirt" (found on the next page and on *The Life of Jesus* DVD) for everyone, and pens or pencils.

Begin by explaining that many times when Jesus wanted to get across a big idea that might have been too difficult for the people to understand, He used a "parable." A parable is a story that communicates a truth in a simple way that people can understand.

Ask for volunteers to read Matthew 13:1-23 to the group, but don't explain the parable until after the activity. Distribute "Getting the Latest Dirt" and pens or pencils. Explain to students that you want them to ask a different student in the room one question each from the handout. If you have a small class, make sure that adults get in on the action.

When students are done interviewing, have them gather in the center of the meeting room and sit down. Ask students to share the answers they collected on their handouts. Have them discuss the following questions:

1. What does Jesus mean when He speaks about soil? *He's making an analogy. The soil is supposed to be our hearts.*

2. What does the seed represent? *God's Word, God's voice.*

3. What is Jesus trying to communicate to His hearers? *God wants us to listen to Him. God wants us to be open to what He has to say to us and obey Him.*

4. Why should we listen to God? *Because God loves us and is the source of our lives. He wants only good things for us and from us.*

Suggest that God strongly desires not only to speak to us, but also longs for us to listen to what He says. The key to communicating with God is removing the things in our lives that prevent us from hearing what He has to say.

GETTING THE LATEST DIRT

1. Ask one person one of the following questions (your choice):

    *   *Who do you think represents the farmer in the story?*

    *   *What do you think the seeds stand for in the story?*

2. Find another person and ask him or her to answer one of these two questions:

    *   *What do you think is the meaning of the rocky soil?*

    *   *Why does Jesus call some soil "rocky"?*

3. You're probably tired, but ask another person one of the following questions:

    *   *Why does Jesus use the example of thorny ground?*

    *   *What do the thorns represent?*

4. You're not done yet? Ask another person—well, you know the drill:

    *   *What do you think the hard ground on the path represents?*

    *   *What do you think the birds represent?*

5. Finally! This is it! Ask one last person one of the following questions:

    *   *Jesus talks about "good soil." What do you think good spiritual soil is?*

    *   *Why is being good soil so important?*

DIG

Option 1: How to Listen to God. You need butcher paper or newsprint, pens or pencils and masking or transparent tape.

Ahead of time, ask several people on your church staff or several close friends to respond to the following statement: "What does it really mean to listen to God?" Write each of their answers on separate large sheets of butcher paper or newsprint, and then tape them to the walls of the meeting room.

At the meeting, explain that you want students to vote in the next few minutes. Point out the statements that you have taped to the walls and ask them to move to the statement that they *most* agree with. When all of the students in your group have decided, have a few of them at each statement share why they've chosen that statement. Then ask students to gather at the statements that they *least* agree with and have them discuss with the whole group why they disagree.

Divide students into groups of three or four and instruct them to think of a new way they could listen to God. Point out that most of us know that we can listen to God in prayer, but you would like for the students to think of other ways we can listen to God, such as walking on the beach or sitting quietly in their room with no music or TV. Be creative.

Allow groups a few minutes to brainstorm, then have each group create a freeze-frame picture that shows their best idea in action, without saying out loud what the picture is. For example, if students think up the idea of walking at the beach as a way to listen to God, include one person walking, another person as the sun and the third person as a wave. When a group has made their presentation, have the other groups guess what they are acting out. *Option*: If you are short on time, you could have each group share their best idea instead of creating a freeze-frame.

Option 2: Learning to Listen. You need one copy of the three "Learning to Listen" worksheets (found on the next three pages and on *The Life of Jesus* DVD) for every five students.

Introduce this section by explaining that listening to God is a daily thing. You're going to look at three daily occurrences in the lives of people who might be hearing God speak to them.

Have students form groups of five; then distribute "Learning to Listen." Ask each group to choose (or you assign) one of the three situations to discuss. Instruct groups to create a simple role-play that would finish these situations. Give groups 3 to 5 minutes, then have each group act out their response.

LEARNING TO LISTEN

SITUATION 1

Lately you've been feeling very out of it—especially at church. When you're there, you feel like they're talking way over your head. It doesn't seem to mean anything to you. And when you read your Bible, you feel like it's written in another language.

And yet you distinctly remember a time when you knew God very well. While you don't consider yourself a spiritual rocket scientist, you're realizing more and more that you don't even remember what God's voice sounds like. You're beyond nervous and approaching worried. Life-changing questions begin creeping up: *Why do I feel so out of touch at church? Why do I feel so distant from God?*

Discuss the following:

• How should this person get back in touch with God?

• How should this person begin listening to God?

LEARNING TO LISTEN

SITUATION 2

You're approached by Jim, Steve and Mary, and they look like they want to talk. You aren't really surprised. The assault begins.

Mary starts in, "Hey, we've been missing you at church lately."

"Yeah, I know. I just feel so bad about going back."

"I wouldn't give it a second thought. I think they've forgotten about when you overflowed the toilet in the restroom. I think they knew you were just goofing off. I wouldn't worry about it."

"Okay, well, maybe."

"So . . . why won't you come back? You know we're having that all-nighter this weekend."

"I just don't know. It's just that ever since that whole thing, I feel like I'm not cut out for church. I think all that heaven stuff is neat, but it doesn't really have anything to do with my life."

Discuss the following:

- Do you think this perseon should consider these friends as God speaking to him? Explain.

- How would you advise this person about listening to God?

LEARNING TO LISTEN

SITUATION 3

Last night you had the weirdest dream that seemed so real.

You dreamed that you were with God in a hallway and He was carrying you. As He held you, you began firing questions at Him about everything you could think of. And the cool thing was that He had the perfect answer to every question you asked. Your last memory in the dream was Him saying to you, "Stand firm, and tell people about Me." Then you woke up.

Well, you did what you thought God told you to do. You told your older brother. After he finished laughing uncontrollably, he said, "You're nuts. No one can hear God, no matter how hard they listen."

So now the ball is directly in your court. How will you respond to your brother? Is it true that you can actually hear God? How will you explain that to him?

Discuss the following:

- Do you think it is true that people can actually hear God?

- Are dreams a real way that God speaks to us?

APPLY

Option 1: Interference. You need Popsicle sticks and fine-tipped felt pens.

Hand each student a Popsicle stick and a pen. Explain that listening to God can be very difficult, especially when there are other distractions going on in our lives. Then ask students to write one thing on their sticks that disrupts their ability to hear God. Answers may include their busy schedules, their friends or their lack of desire. Collect the sticks and then toss them all in the air, letting them fall to the floor. Ask students to grab one of the sticks that isn't theirs and read it to themselves. Explain that you want them to pair up and come up with a solution to the problem that's written on the stick.

Give the pairs 2 or 3 minutes to discuss, then explain that the best way to hear God is by having a personal relationship with Him. Share how your personal relationship with Jesus has affected your life, and then give students an opportunity to ask Jesus to be their Savior, take over their lives and speak to them just as a best friend would.

Option 2: What I Need to Do. Remind students that God wants us to listen to Him. He wants our hearts to be open and ready to hear what He has to say. If possible, share a story about a time you needed to change some things in your life to help students start thinking about the choice they're about to make.

Explain that the left side of the room is the "I need to listen" side, for people who don't have many things in their lives that might distract them from hearing God—they just need to listen. The right side of the room is the "I need to clean house" side, for people who have some work to do before they will be able to listen. They need to get rid of the rocks and thorns that distract them from listening to or even recognizing God's voice. Assure students that they're *not* being graded on their spirituality or their relationship with God. Turn off (or dim) the lights. Instruct students to walk to whichever side of the room describes them best. If students aren't sure, have them stand in the center.

Spend the next several minutes allowing students to pray aloud for each other in pairs where they are standing. Then close the meeting with prayer, asking God to encourage students as they strive to listen to what He wants to say to them. *Hint*: junior-highers (and many adults!) are hesitant to make tough decisions in front of their friends. They are more likely to take the plunge if they see others making big choices. If you have other adult leaders or volunteers, ask them to respond, too. If you are the sole adult, you should respond. Seeing adults admit to these rocks or thorns will encourage students to be more comfortable with responding.

REFLECT

The following short devotions are for the students to reflect on and answer during the week. You can make a copy of these pages and distribute to your class or print out from the PDF for this session found on *The Life of Jesus* DVD.

1—OUT OF LOVE

Get into 1 John 5:1-4 to see if God's commandments are heavy or light.

Every night, Evan had to clean the kitchen. On Thursday, Evan and his mom had a great day together—they rented a video and made sundaes for dessert. That night Evan finished cleaning the kitchen in 20 minutes.

The next day, Evan fought with his mom over using the phone and was so busy thinking about how unfair his mother was that it took him an hour and a half to clean the kitchen.

Why do you think it took Evan so much longer on the second night?

_____

_____

_____

_____

Lots of times it's easier to obey someone and do the right thing when you remember how much you love the person in charge. Doing what God wants you to do is way easier to do when you're in love with Him. What are two things that would be different in your week if you were in love with God?

2—THE RIGHT TOOLS

Run—don't walk!—to 2 Timothy 1:7 and discover some of the things God has given to you.

If you were going to dissect a frog in science class, which of these tools would your teacher give you? (Check all that apply.)

- ❐ A white lab coat
- ❐ A box of 50 blue ballpoint pens
- ❐ A scalpel and tweezers
- ❐ A hairbrush

According to 2 Timothy 1:7, what tools has God given you that will help you follow Him?

_____

_____

_____

_____

_____

What are some of the ways you can use the tools God has given you today?

_____

_____

_____

_____

_____

3—EYES IN THE BACK OF HIS HEAD

Flip to Psalm 119:166-168 to find out how much God knows about you.

Mai was supposed to be vacuuming her mother's bedroom. But she wasn't. She was poking around in her mother's makeup, putting lipstick on her mouth and mascara on her eyelashes. She dug in the dresser drawer and found her mother's favorite necklace. As she went to put it on, she looked in the mirror and saw her mother standing behind her, watching her with arms crossed.

God is a lot like the parent with eyes in the back of His head. The only difference is that God really does know all about you and He knows what's best for you.

The best way to let God take care of you is to obey His commandments. He has given us these commandments to protect us. He knows you better than anyone—and He loves you better than anyone!

What is one of His commandments that you could obey today that you didn't obey yesterday? How?

_____

_____

_____

_____

_____

4—WHO TO FOLLOW

See how fast you can find 1 Corinthians 11:1. Time yourself, and then find out whose example you should be following.

If you were lost at Disneyland and could only follow one person to an exit, who would you follow? Would it be . . .

- ❏ The girl selling churros and frozen lemonade?
- ❏ A four-year-old crying for his blanket?
- ❏ Your mom or dad?
- ❏ A person dressed up in a Donald Duck suit who can't see very well?

Why would you follow that person?

_____

_____

_____

_____

In this life, why is Jesus the right Person to follow?

_____

_____

_____

_____

What do you think He might lead you to do today?

_____

_____

_____

_____

FAITH

THE BIG IDEA
A little faith goes a long way.

SESSION AIMS
In this session you will guide students to (1) see that even little faith makes a big difference; (2) feel comforted knowing that they can accomplish great things if they have faith; and (3) choose one area in their lives where they would like to have more faith.

THE BIGGEST VERSE
"I tell you the truth, if you have faith as small as a mustard seed. . . . Nothing will be impossible for you" (Matthew 17:20).

OTHER IMPORTANT VERSES
Matthew 17:14-21; Hebrews 11:1-2; James 1:2-4

STARTER

Option 1: Foot Lineup. You need your Bible, one or two large bedsheets, paper and pens or pencils.

Ahead of time, ask five students to volunteer for a foot-identification game. Tell them that when the game starts, you'd like them to take off their shoes and socks and roll up their pants so that their clothes don't show beneath the sheet they will be standing behind.

At the meeting, greet students and instruct them to gather at one end of the meeting room. Distribute a piece of paper and a pen or pencil to each student. Ask two students or adult leaders to volunteer to hold the bedsheet approximately one foot off the ground like a curtain, then ask everyone to close their eyes. When everyone has done so, ask the barefoot volunteers to enter and stand behind the bedsheet. Before you have students open their eyes, make sure that only the volunteers' feet are visible.

Ask students to open their eyes and then ask students to guess who is standing on the other side of the sheet, and write down their guesses. Number the feet 1 to 5.

When everyone has guessed, have the two volunteers drop the sheet. Have students check their answers by pointing out each set and asking students to stand if they guessed correctly. When everyone has shared his or her guess, ask the following:

- How many of you were sure about your guesses?
- What made you sure about your guesses?
- What made this activity difficult?
- What would have made it easier?

Read Hebrews 11:1 and then ask students how they think this passage relates to the game that they just played. Explain that having faith is a lot like this game. You couldn't see who was behind the sheet except for their feet, which were evidence of the actual person. Our faith is like that. We can't see all of God, but we can figure out how He is working. And today you're going to learn more about how to know where God is working even though we can't see Him.

Option 2: Faith Statements. You need several Bibles, large sheets of newsprint or poster board, masking or transparent tape and several felt-tip pens.

Ahead of time, write the following statements on the sheets of paper; then hang the papers on the wall in various locations around the room:

- All of us get faith as a gift when we give our lives to Christ.
- Jesus only intended some of us to be able to do amazing things with faith.
- Since you really can't see faith, it doesn't exist.
- Jesus was able to do miracles, but He doesn't expect that we will be able to do them.

At the meeting, welcome students and have them form groups of three. Give each group a felt-tip pen. Instruct students to walk to each statement and write on the paper whether they—as a group—agree or disagree with the statement and why. When all groups have had a chance to write their responses, ask students to leave their groups and go to the statement that they feel they *individually* agree with the most. After students have chosen their statements, give these new groups (standing at each statement) five minutes to come up with a way to defend that statement.

When groups are finished, have them present their defenses and be sure to congratulate everyone on their hard work. Then read Hebrews 11:1 and ask the following questions (based on the *New King James Version*):

- What does it mean when it says that faith is "the substance of things hoped for"?
- What does it mean when it says that faith is "the evidence of things not seen"?
- Is it difficult for you to prove something you can't see?
- What does it take to believe in something that you can't see?

Explain that today you'll be talking about faith—something that we can't see, but we sure can see what it does in our lives.

MESSAGE

Option 1: Faith the Size of a Toothpick. You need several bags of large marshmallows (20 marshmallows for every four to six students), a box or two of toothpicks (20 toothpicks for every four to six students), several Bibles, paper and pens or pencils.

Divide students into small groups of four to six and give each group 20 marshmallows. Next, ask the students to build the tallest tower they can, using just the marshmallows. Let them attempt it for a minute or two. This will be very frustrating until you hand each group 20 toothpicks; then they can really begin to build a tall tower. When they're finished, judge which tower is the tallest. Comment on the fact that although toothpicks seem to be small and unimportant, they make the marshmallow towers possible.

Next, read Matthew 17:14-21 and point out that the amazing thing Jesus does in this passage is heal the boy. But the *point* of it is that Jesus wants us to understand how essential faith is in the life of the believer. Now ask students to imagine for a moment that they are present in this situation.

Assign each small group one of the following people to represent: the boy's father, the disciples, part of the crowd, the boy. Give each group paper and pens or pencils. Have groups write a first-person story based on their assigned person's perspective as they watch Jesus heal the boy. When everyone is finished writing, have each small group read their story to another group. Then bring the students together to share with the whole group what they learned about the situation in Matthew as a result of this activity.

Now discuss the following questions:

1. What does this passage say about faith? *Even a small amount of faith can do what seems impossible to us.*[1]

2. How are we supposed to show faith? *By putting our trust in Jesus' power to accomplish great things.*

3. What is difficult about doing the miraculous things that Jesus says we can do? *They are seemingly impossible and we know we can't do them on our own. But the Bible is full of the miraculous things God did when someone had a little faith.*

4. What are the essential ingredients for faith? *Trust. Hope.*

Youth Leader Tip

When you feel you aren't communicating with your group, try exaggerating everything you are saying. Shout directions. Stand on your head. Or just hang on—sometimes kids aren't following you, but they haven't given up yet. Only stop a lesson if you're sure they've checked out.

5. Why does Jesus equate faith to the size of a mustard seed? *He wants us to understand that we need just a little faith to do great things. A mustard seed is very small and yet it can grow into a huge bush.*

Suggest that faith is an interesting thing: We can't see it, but we can see the effects of it. It was impossible to "see" the faith that Jesus had to be able to heal the boy, but the effects of His work were obvious. Jesus told us that if *we* have faith, *we* can do amazing things. He promised us that nothing would be impossible for us if we have faith. Now it's time to focus on how we can have faith even when we can't see it.

Option 2: Faith Experiment. You need several Bibles, vegetable oil, a clear glass half full of water, one-fourth cup of salt and a small bottle of food coloring.

Ahead of time, practice this "experiment" to be able to talk about it and perform the actions at the same time. At the meeting, gather students in the center of the room as you explain that little things can make a big difference— and you've got a little experiment today to prove it.

Show the glass of water. Pour some vegetable oil into the glass and allow it to separate from the water. Next, put two drops of food coloring into the water and wait for it to drop out of the oil and into the water. Explain that a little bit of food coloring can make a big difference in the water. Next, sprinkle salt on the top of the oil, making sure to distribute the salt evenly over the surface of the oil. Allow time for the salt to sink the oil to the bottom, and the oil to rise to the surface again. Conclude by asking students to explain what they are seeing. Confirm that a little bit of salt or a little bit of food coloring makes a big difference.

In the same way, Jesus explained that even a little bit of faith could make a big difference. Read Matthew 17:14-21. Now discuss the following:

- What would you be thinking if you were a disciple and saw this happen?
- What would you think if you were the boy?
- What if you were the boy's parents?
- If you were a disciple, would you want to be able to do what Jesus did?

Read Matthew 17:20-21 again and ask:

1. Why does Jesus compare faith to a mustard seed? *Because a mustard seed is very small, but it can grow into a huge bush. Jesus wants*

us to understand that all we need is a small amount of faith to do great
things for God and our faith will grow.

2. Why do you think Jesus used the example of moving a mountain to
   show the power of faith? *Because He wants us to know that even big*
   things are no problem if we have faith.

Ask students to imagine hearing Jesus' words for the first time. Wouldn't
their reaction be one of wonder and amazement? Now ask them to imagine
hearing Him say that they could move mountains.

Faith might be invisible, but the effects of faith in our lives are certainly clear
to see. God has called us to have faith and next you're going to figure out together how to use it.

DIG

Option 1: Faith in the Real World. You need several Bibles and copies of "Faith
in the Real World" (found on the next three pages and on *The Life of Jesus* DVD).

Explain that all this faith you've been talking about can be somewhat difficult to have. To make it easier, you'd like students to consider how they can
have faith when they are in the middle of a crisis.

Divide students into three groups and assign each group one of the situations from "Faith in the Real World." Ask the groups to read their situations and
discuss how they could exercise faith in that situation. Allow enough time for
each group to prepare their explanation, then have them share their situations
and ideas with the whole group. Discuss the following questions:

1. Does God expect that we'll always be successful in living our faith
   and performing miracles? *He'd like us to be full of faith, but He knows*
   that we all fail at times. (Suggestion: Give a personal example of how
   your own faith has faltered.) Whenever we lack faith, we can ask Him
   to give us faith.

2. What should we do when we feel like we have faith but nothing
   happens? *Keep praying and trusting God to do what is best. If we have*
   faith that God will do something, such as giving us the latest, greatest
   bike, when that's not His will, then He won't do it. But He will do and
   give what is best for us.

FAITH IN THE REAL WORLD

SITUATION ONE

You've been your grandma's favorite since you were born. When you were a small child, the two of you spent countless hours watching television game shows together, competing for who could get the right answers. As you got older, your grandma was always a source of encouragement and wisdom.

Last night, someone from the hospital called. It seems that as your grandma was sitting down for dinner, she began to complain of a headache and then fell unconscious. Paramedics were called and they rushed her to the hospital, where it was determined that she had experienced a severe stroke. Her mental faculties are all but gone and the doctors say she only has a few days to live.

You're standing over her as she lies helpless in her hospital bed. You feel led to pray for a complete healing.

- How does Matthew 17:20-21 help you understand your role in your grandmother's healing?

- How can you have faith in the middle of this situation?

- Is it right for you to expect that she will be healed? Explain.

- If she isn't healed, what is the best attitude to have toward God?

FAITH IN THE REAL WORLD

SITUATION TWO

Since you were five years old, your father has been an independent businessman. When he began his business, it took off immediately. The boom in his business meant that your family was able to have the best of everything. There were frequent trips to Hawaii, new cars, the latest clothes and scores of other benefits.

But recently his business hasn't been going so well. In fact, business has been very slow. This year your family isn't going anywhere for vacation. If things don't change, it looks like your dad will have to take on a second job at a local grocery store to make ends meet.

Tonight your dad broke all of this news at the dinner table. He says that the family needs to have faith that God will meet the needs that you and your family have.

- How might Matthew 17:20-21 help you live through this difficult time with your family?

- How can you have faith in the middle of this situation?

- If your father's business fails even more, does that mean that you didn't have enough faith? Explain.

- Read James 1:2-4. What should you completely trust God for?

FAITH IN THE REAL WORLD

SITUATION THREE

Your older sister has always been the popular one in the family. She's been on the cheerleading squad since she started high school, as well as the drama team at your church. She always seems to have a boyfriend. You love your sister, but you're also jealous of her popularity and abilities. You wish you could be just like her.

But you feel like the family ugly duckling. Even though you're just three years younger, you don't have the friends that she has. You aren't as smart as she is. You can't sing, dance or act like she does. Last night you sat on your bed and just cried. You want so much to be like her, but you feel so awkward and you're convinced that you'll be just a "plain old ordinary nothing" forever.

Your mom heard you crying and came in to check on you. After spilling your guts, your mom told you that you needed to trust God for what He is creating you to be. God is creating you to be something incredible (so your mom says), but finding out what that is takes time.

Your mom's words are comforting, but they don't help you as much as you need them to.

- How does Matthew 17:20-21 help you wait on God?

- How can you have faith in the middle of this situation?

- If you don't turn out like your sister, is it because you didn't have enough faith?

- Read James 1:2-4. What should you completely trust God for?

Option 2: To Drink or Not to Drink. For this option, you will need several Bibles. Introduce this option by asking students to listen to a story that shows us how to have faith.

Many years ago, a weary traveler hiked for miles across the desert with the hot sun beating down on him. His water supply was gone and he knew that if he didn't find water soon to quench his thirst, he would surely die.

In the distance, he spotted a deserted cabin, which gave him hope that maybe water could be found there. He made his way to the cabin and discovered an old well. He frantically pumped the handle of the well to draw water, but all that came from the pump was dust.

Then he noticed a tin can tied to the pump, with a note inside. The note said: "Dear stranger: This pump is all right as of June 1932. I put a new sucker washer in it, and it should last for quite a few years. But the washer dries out and the pump needs to be primed.

"Under the white rock, I buried a jar of water, out of the sun and corked up. There's enough water in it to prime the pump, but not if you drink some first. Pour about one-fourth of the water into the pump and let her soak for a minute to wet the leather washer. Then pour the rest quickly and pump hard. You'll get water. Have faith. This well has never run dry. When you get watered up, fill the bottle and put it back as you found it for the next stranger who comes this way.

—Pete"[1]

Next, discuss the following questions:

- Would you pour the water into the pump or drink the water? Why?
- Why is it difficult to have faith in something that we can't see?
- What does this story tell you about faith?

Explain that sometimes we might have to do something or trust something that seems unrealistic or just plain dumb before we get results. Having faith means that we trust God no matter what. Sometimes believing that God wants to use us to do miraculous things is like pouring out water without knowing if our experiment will work.

Next, help students get a broader view of what the Bible says about faith by having them read Hebrews 11:1 and James 1:5-8.

APPLY

Option 1: Tearing Down Obstacles to Faith. You need molding clay or play dough, worship music, a trashcan and a large plastic trash bag.

Explain that you'd like students to take a moment to think about what stops them from having the type of faith that Jesus talks about.

Distribute molding clay or play dough and give students 3 to 5 minutes to make their clay into something that represents what they feel is a barrier preventing them from having mountain-moving faith. When students are done, ask them to choose a partner with whom to share their sculptures. Allow students a few minutes to share what their sculptures represent.

Next, ask students to commit their barriers to God. Let them know that you're going to give them some time to talk with Him and ask His help in removing their barriers. If they finish praying before the music stops, they should sit quietly and think about what you've talked about today. Play some quiet worship music for 2 or 3 minutes as the students pray silently.

When the music is over, have students demonstrate their commitments by coming forward, smashing their sculptures and dropping them on the floor. (*Note*: Keep peace with the custodian and place the plastic trash bag on the floor where students will be dropping the clay.) As students drop their clay, begin to form it into one huge ball. When all the clay has been dropped, throw it in the trashcan as a symbol of faith that God will remove those obstacles. Close the meeting with prayer asking God to remove their obstacles.

Option 2: Sharing the Good News. You need a clear two-liter bottle of soda, seven clear plastic cups, a funnel and a table.

Ahead of time, set up the table and place the bottle and plastic cups on the table. Pour the contents of the soda bottle into the seven plastic cups.

Explain that having faith in God means we that have faith that He can use us to share His Good News with our friends. Sometimes we feel bad when we share with our friends and nothing happens, but the reality is that something *is*

Youth Leader Tip

Any time you give students the opportunity to ask Jesus to take over their lives and be their Savior, make sure that you follow up with them. Contact them within three days to talk with them about their decision, and offer to give them a Bible if they don't have one.

probably happening, even if we can't see it. Studies show that the average junior-higher receives Christ after he or she has heard about Him seven times.

At this point, point to your clear bottle and explain that the bottle represents a junior-higher named Doug. *First, you invite Doug to church.* Pour one glass of soda back into the bottle representing Doug. *Next, Doug's aunt sends him a Christmas card that explains the gospel message.* Pour another glass of soda into Doug. Continue to pour the remaining five glasses of sodas as you add additional scenarios of how Doug might hear about Jesus, such as *Doug goes to church with a new friend; Doug watches a Christian television show; one of Doug's teachers tells him that he's praying for him; Doug asks you to explain about a sticker for a Christian band that you have on your notebook; and Doug hears Christian music on your stereo and says he can't figure out what the words mean.*

Now the bottle representing Doug should be full. Explain that at this point, Doug is ready to receive Christ as Savior. Continue by suggesting that we never know what role we are playing in our friends' process of coming to know Jesus. We may be the first or we may be the third time they hear about Him. The important thing is to continue to have faith that God will use us.

Close in prayer, asking students to pray in pairs for two other friends or relatives they know who don't know Christ yet. Ask them to ask God to give them faith and courage to share with these two people.

REFLECT

The following short devotions are for the students to reflect on and answer during the week. You can make a copy of these pages and distribute to your class or print out from the PDF for this session found on *The Life of Jesus* DVD.

1—FAITH: WHERE DO YOU GET IT?

Read Mark 9:14-29 and find out what's possible!

Your grandma has had cancer for as long as you can remember. Every night at dinner your mom prays that God will heal her. After all these years, you're getting tired of hearing that prayer. If God were going to heal Grandma, wouldn't He have done it already? One night as you're staring at some tuna casserole and hearing your mom pray the same prayer yet again, you realize how wrong you have been. If you decided that you wanted to pray with the same kind of faith that your mom has, should you . . .

- ❏ Sleep with a Bible under your pillow so faith can drift into your mind?
- ❏ Make up a song about faith that you sing under your breath as much as possible?
- ❏ Decide to change your name to "Faith" to constantly remind yourself of your need for faith?
- ❏ Ask God for it?

The example of the father who confessed to Jesus, "I believe! Help my lack of faith!" answers the question. If you don't feel you have faith when you pray, whether it be for your sick grandma or your neighbor who doesn't know Jesus yet, you can ask God for it. In His timing, He'll give it to you. Then you'll see some out-of-this-world things happening around you when you pray!

2—YOUR WILL BE DONE

Read Matthew 21:18-22 and be glad you're not a figless fig tree!

Maria prayed for weeks and weeks and weeks that her parents would get her a new cell phone. Across town, Clara wanted the same thing but prayed only that God's will would be done. Two months passed and neither of them got new cell phones. *That's not fair!* Maria thought, *Jesus made a fig tree shrivel up, and He said I could have anything if I just had faith!*

Clara was just as disappointed at not getting what she wanted, but because of her faith, she knew that God's will was the important thing. It's easy to think that today's verses mean we can have anything we want just by having enough faith. But the more faith in God you gain, the more you will want to follow God's will. Take two minutes to pray about one hard or confusing area in your life, asking that God's will be done.

3—HOW HIGH CAN YOU CLIMB?

Race to Romans 1:1-5 to find out what comes with faith.

Imagine that you're rock-climbing for the first time but you're not having much success because:

- You ignored the directions on your harness, so it's loose.
- You were told by the instructor to wear a helmet, but you decided it looked lame.
- You wore flip-flops instead of rock-climbing shoes.
- You skipped the beginning rock-climbing lesson so you could sleep in.

What do you need to do to be prepared to climb with God today?

4—WHERE DO WE START?

See how long it takes you to find 1 Corinthians 16:13. It's so nice, read it twice!

When Mark started mowing Mrs. Barnfeather's lawn, he wanted to know exactly how she wanted it done. Did she want the edges trimmed and the flowerbeds weeded? Did she want him to come every week or every other week? Did she want him to pull the dandelions out or did she want him to spray Weed-B-Gone on them? He asked her a billion questions and wrote down her answers on a little piece of paper.

When Mark became a Christian, he looked at the big, thick Bible his youth pastor gave him and had a billion more questions than he had ever had for Mrs. Barnfeather. But he wasn't sure where to start.

Today's verse is a super-short version of how a Christian should behave. Jesus thinks our faith is one of the most important things we need to grow. Pray that He will help you have a solid faith in Him today—that's where we all need to start!

GIFTED BY GOD

THE BIG IDEA

God has given us some amazing talents that He wants us to use to help others.

SESSION AIMS

In this session you will guide students to (1) recognize the importance of using their gifts; (2) feel encouraged that they have more gifts than they realize; and (3) commit to using the gifts that God has given them to help others this week.

THE BIGGEST VERSE

"Well done, good and faithful servant! You have been faithful with a few things; I will put you in charge of many things. Come and share your master's happiness" (Matthew 25:21).

OTHER IMPORTANT VERSES

Matthew 25:14-30; Romans 12:4-8; 1 Peter 4:10-11

STARTER

Option 1: Hunting for Ways to Serve. You need paper, envelopes, pens or pencils and candy prizes for the winning team.

Ahead of time, design a team scavenger hunt related to various locations throughout the church facilities. For example, one clue could be something like "If you've just finished playing football, you're probably going to run to this" (water fountain), or "If you like to read, this will be one of your favorite places" (the church library). Be sure to have 8 to 10 locations for the students to track down. Put clues to each location in a separate envelope for each team. There should be enough envelopes for the number of groups of eight that you think you will have. Label each of the envelopes by team number and rearrange the order of the clues for each team so that the teams don't keep bumping into each other (or cheat by following each other!). Distribute the clues in labeled envelopes around the church facility so that as a team reaches the correct destination, it finds another clue.

At the meeting, greet students and explain that today you're going to start off with a scavenger hunt in the church. Divide students into teams of no more than eight. (*Note*: If you have a youth group of fewer than 16, just divide them in half.) Give each team a pen or pencil, a piece of paper and their first envelope. Instruct them to use the clue in the envelope to arrive at a location somewhere in the church facility. Tell students that when they reach the correct location, they will find a clue to the next place in an envelope marked with their team number.

As they arrive at each place, have students write down three ways someone could use their gifts and talents to serve God and others who come to that location. For example, if the clue leads them to the church nursery they could write down "The nursery: *caring* for babies, *teaching* them about God's love, *serving* parents by caring for their children."

Once the groups return, congratulate the winning team (the one who finished first) and ask students to identify what all of the scavenger hunt locations

Youth Leader Tip

To help junior-highers feel comfortable in using their gifts from God, try offering programs that will get them involved in their passions, or be their advocate in encouraging them to use their gifts and abilities in your church and your local community.

had in common. (They were all places where we use the special talents or abilities that God has given us.) Then let them know that today they're going to learn how to use their talents, whatever they may be, in the best ways possible.

Option 2: Would You Rather Be? You need just this book.

Welcome students and explain that they're going to play "Would You Rather Be?" As you read a pair of choices, students will move to the side of the room that indicates their choice. If they'd rather be the first type of person, they should move to the left side of the room. If they'd rather be the second type of person, they should move to the right side of the room.

Ask the students the following question: *Would you rather be . . .*

- *A brilliant computer scientist or a fantastic runway model?*
- *The world's best skateboarder or the world's best snow skier?*
- *A dancer in a football halftime show or a football player in the game?*
- *Able to burp the alphabet or able to walk on your hands?*
- *An elementary school teacher or a writer of children's books?*
- *The best player on your soccer team or the best student in your school?*

Ask students if they can figure out what all of these have in common. The answer is that they are all talents. Explain that a talent is a special ability and as followers of Jesus, we know that God gives us our talents. Today, they're going to learn more about how to use their talents in the best way possible.

MESSAGE

Option 1: Cool Questions. You need several Bibles and one copy of "Cool Questions" (found on the next page and on *The Life of Jesus* DVD). Ahead of time, cut the "Cool Questions" handout into eight separate questions and tape each question to the bottom of a different chair in the meeting room.

At the meeting, read Matthew 25:14-30 aloud, and then explain that although a talent was a type of money in Jesus' day, today we can interpret it as a special ability or gift.[1] Explain that you're going to play a game to help them look closer at the passage.

Ask students to put their chairs in a circle, facing inward. Divide students into four different groups, labeling each group a different animal name, such as "Armadillo," "Squid," "Platypus" and "Sloth." Then have students move and find new seats, making sure that they are not sitting next to anyone else from

Cool Questions

1. Who does the master represent?	2. Who do the servants represent?
3. What does the talent represent?	4. What does the master think of the guy with five talents and the guy with two talents?
5. Why did the master get angry with the last servant?	6. What happened to the servant who didn't do anything with his talent?
7. Which servant do you relate to the most?	8. How would you summarize the meaning of this parable in one sentence?

their same animal group. Ask one student to stand in the middle of the circle and remove her chair.

Explain that the person in the middle of the circle is going to yell two or more different types of animals. The students who are in those animal groups must stand up and run to find new chairs. The person in the middle of the circle must also find an empty chair. The person left without a chair then stands in the middle of the circle and the process is repeated.

After a few people have been in the middle of the circle, ask students to look under their chairs for Question 1. Tell students to leave all the other questions taped to the bottom of the chairs. Whoever finds Question 1 must take it off the chair, stand up, read the question aloud and try to answer it. Other members of that person's same animal group may also help.

Once they have answered correctly, play a few more rounds of the game, then ask students to look under their chairs for Question 2. Repeat this process until all eight questions have been answered. (Answers: (1) God. (2) Us. (3) An ability, skill or gift. (4) He congratulated them for a job well done. (5) Because the servant didn't use his one talent to do any good. (6) The servant lost his talent. (7) Answers will vary. (8) God wants us to use every gift He has given us, or we might lose them.)

Conclude with the following discussion:

- What does God expect us to do with talents that He gives us?
- What happens if we don't?

Option 2: God's Gifts. You need your Bible, a book or box of matches, a metal pan, a table or other surface to set the pan on and a sheet of paper.

Ahead of time, set up the table at the front of the room and place the metal pan on it. *Campfire Option:* Prepare wood for a campfire or in a fireplace; then during the third point of the talk, light the fire—further illustrating the point of using your gifts to serve others.

At the meeting, tell the students that we should do four things with the gifts God gives us:

1. *Receive the gift.* Read Matthew 25:14-30 to the group and ask if they think this is a story about an angry master who just wants to stick it to his servants. Suggest that instead, the master wants the best for his servants. He's not trying to catch them doing something wrong—he wants to challenge them to use what they have

been given in a responsible way. Explain that the master represents God, and the story explains what God expects us to do with the gifts He has given us.

2. *Recognize the gift.* Explain that the wicked, lazy servant didn't recognize his talent as an incredible gift that the owner had given him, so he hid it. The bottom line is that we need to recognize what God has given us. Hold up the match and ask, "What do I have in my hand?" Students will (hopefully!) say, "A match." But what if you didn't think it was a match at all? You thought it was just a stick with a dirty tip. You have the potential for fire in your hand, but because you don't understand what you have and refuse to discover what it is, you will miss out on something important. If we were cold and needed to start a fire to warm up, you would have the potential to do that right here in your hand. But if you don't know what you've got, it does us no good. Just like a gift or a special ability: If you don't use it, it's worthless.

3. *Use the gift.* Explain that knowing what we've been given by God can be a huge step. But if we stop there, we run the risk of being poor stewards or caretakers of what we have. Light the match and place it in the metal pan. As it burns, tell students all of the things that you might do with this fire. While the match slowly burns out, lead them to understand that simply lighting the match isn't enough; we have to actually use it to set something on fire before it can be useful to us.

4. *Serve with the gift.* Explain that the chief goal of the gifts that God has given us is to serve others and help them know Him. God has given us incredible gifts. These gifts have the potential to do marvelous things for God's kingdom—if we'll learn what gifts we have and then use them to help others. Hold up the match and the piece of paper. Light the match, then use it to light the paper. Tell students that this is exactly what we need to do with the gifts that God gives us: use them! *Note:* If you are doing the Campfire Option, use the paper to light the wood in the campfire or fireplace. Point out how lighting the match has made it possible to start the fire that warms everyone around it.

DIG

Option 1: The Right Equipment. You need four copies of "The Right Equipment" (found on the next three pages and on *The Life of Jesus* DVD) and the props listed on the script.

Ahead of time, ask four students to act out "The Right Equipment" and give them copies of the skit so that they can practice their parts.

At the meeting, explain that the drama students are about to see represents many people's view about using the talents God has given them. Invite the actors to present the skit.

After the drama is acted out, ask the group the following:

- Which of these people did you relate to the most?
- When have you refused to use one of God's gifts?

Explain that Jesus' parable doesn't give a lot of specific ideas on how we're supposed to use our talents, but Paul does. Read Romans 12:4-8. (*Note*: Make sure students understand that this is not a comprehensive list and that they might have gifts that aren't listed.) Now ask:

- Where does God want us to use our talents?
- What talents has God given you?
- How do you think He wants you to use them?
- According to today's story, what happens if we choose not to use our talents?

Read 1 Peter 4:10 aloud and challenge students to consider how they can use at least one of their talents to faithfully minister God's grace to others—in a way that shows something about who God is and how much He cares about others. How can they use their gifts to serve in the youth group?

Youth Leader Tip

Another way to get your students involved in using their gifts is to keep a list of things that you (or others) would love to have done around the church. This way, if a student ever asks you how he or she can help out, you will have some suggestions ready.

THE RIGHT EQUIPMENT

Cast
Josh, a teenager
Skateboarder, carrying a skateboard (of course)
High School Guy, carrying a pair of keys
Girl with Bike, junior-high age

Props
A toolbox, a skateboard, some coins, a set of car keys, a bike and a trash can.

Josh runs on stage carrying a large, shiny toolbox.

Josh: (*Calling backstage.*) Dad! Wait—Dad! Hold up, will ya? You forgot your toolbox! (*Trying to catch his breath.*) No, you forgot it. (*Stops.*) What do you mean? Wait. Time out. What do I want with this thing? No, no, Dad, it's your toolbox. Awww, is this one of those "You're a man now, you need your own toolbox" routines? Okay, so it's mine now. Fine. So how long you gonna be gone? Dad? Dad! (*No reply. He looks at the toolbox.*) This is just great. He couldn't pull the "You're a man now, you need your own 4x4" routine? (*He unlatches the toolbox.*) What am I doing? No way. I touch it and something's gonna break. Guaranteed. (*Locks it down.*) Yeah, if something happens to anything before he gets back, I'll just tell him I didn't touch a pickin' thing. That's my story.

Skateboarder enters from the opposite side of the stage carrying his skateboard. Josh picks up the toolbox and walks past the Skateboarder and tries to ignore him.

Skateboarder: Hey. Hey, dude.
Josh: What do you want? (*Keeps walking.*)
Skateboarder: Wait, wait. My wheels are starting to fall off my board. Got anything that might help?
Josh: (*Rolls his eyes, says sarcastically*) Sure. In my back pocket.
Skateboarder: (*Looking at the toolbox.*) What about the toolbox?
Josh: (*Trying to hide the toolbox behind him.*) What about it?
Skateboarder: Where did you get it?
Josh: My father. What do you care?
Skateboarder: What do you have in it?

Josh: I don't know.

Skateboarder: Ain't ya looked in it even? There might be something in there to help my wheels. Why don't you open it up?

Josh: Trust me. There's nothing that can help you in here!

Skateboarder: Maybe I could use a screwdriver or a hammer or somethin', huh?

Josh: (*Shoving a coin at him.*) Here's some money. Go make a phone call. I'm not opening the toolbox, okay?!

Skateboarder: (*Walks away mumbling.*) Why do ya carry the thing around if ya ain't gonna use it? Sheesh!

High School Guy: (*Calling from offstage.*) Hey, pal! Hey, buddy! (*Josh turns around. He sees High School Guy with keys in his hands.*) Hey, do you think you've got a trimensional dual-sided spanner in that box?

Josh: Say what?

High School Guy: Hey, no, really, do you mind if I take a look? It'd really help me out. My catalytic converter is busted. (*He goes to Josh, who backs away, hugging the toolbox.*)

Josh: You're not looking in my toolbox.

High School Guy: Come on. That's a spiffy box there, I'm broke down, huh? One look. Okay?

Josh: Look! I'm not opening the toolbox! My dad gave it to me. It's his, got it? I'm not gonna use nothin'.

High School Guy: If your dad gave it to ya, then I'm sure he wouldn't mind.

Josh: He minds!

High School Guy: (*Throws his hands up in surrender.*) Okay, okay. Don't get all crazy. (*High School Guy goes out. Girl with Bike comes in behind Josh. Josh sighs and turns around.*)

Girl with Bike: Nice toolbox. You think you got a—

Josh: No!

Girl with Bike: Maybe a wrench or some—

Josh: Nothing!

Girl with Bike: (*Gestures at the box.*) What's that there, then?

Josh: (*Backing away.*) A mistake, that's what it is. Somebody just gave it to me. I didn't know I was going to have to do something with it.

Girl with Bike: Well, hey, can I have it then?

Josh: No! It's mine! Now start walking. (*Girl with Bike doesn't move.*) Unbelievable. I don't need this grief. None of it! (*He looks around and sees a* *garbage can on the other side of the stage. He goes and stuffs the toolbox in it.*) That'll work. When my dad comes back, I'll go get the stupid toolbox for him. He ought to be grateful. It'll all be in one piece when he gets it. (*Pauses. Wipes his hands.*) Yeah, he should be real happy I took no-o-o chances with it.

Josh taps the garbage can twice and goes out, hands stuffed in his pockets.[2]

Option 2: Tools for the Job. For this option, you will need a comb, a shoe, an eraser and masking tape.

Ask for four volunteers. One at a time, give each of the volunteers one of the four items listed above. Explain that they are to use the given object to act out whatever you whisper in their ear while the rest of the group tries to guess what they are doing. Here are the actions you will tell the volunteers:

- A comb being used to sweep the floor
- A shoe being used to spread and then toss pizza dough
- An eraser being used to clean hands.
- A piece of tape being used to handcuff a prisoner

After volunteers have acted out all four scenarios and the rest of the students have guessed the actions, ask the students what was wrong with using these objects this way. Then explain to the group that it is important for each of us to figure out how to use every talent God gives us in the right way, or we're going to be ineffective.

Jesus' parable doesn't give a lot of specific ideas about how we're supposed to use our talents, but Paul does. Read Romans 12:4-8 to show some of the ways we can use our talents. (*Note*: Make sure students understand that this is not a comprehensive list and that they might have gifts that aren't listed.)

Youth Leader Tip

If you don't have time to give students this skit in advance, try making up cue cards and have them just read their parts off the cards. Or make up "gist" cards—cue cards that just direct them on the story of the skit and cue the actors on their emotions and movements.

Discuss the following:

1. What does it mean that we "belong" to each other? *It means that we are all part of the Body of Christ.*

2. How does each ability contribute to the Body? *By serving others and helping them know more about Jesus.*

Read 1 Peter 4:10-11, and then ask the following:

1. How does it feel to know that you can use your gift to administer God's grace to others?

2. What does it mean to use your gift faithfully? It means that we must use it whenever we see a need or feel "called" to use it.

3. What are some gifts that can be used in our youth ministry right here and now?

Explain to students that it's essential for them to discover the talents God has given them. (If they are unsure about what their gifts are, you might want to use a spiritual gifts test or some further teaching on this subject in the future.) Help students understand that everything that God gives us can be used to serve others.

APPLY

Option 1: Catching an Airplane. You need paper and pens or pencils.

Explain that since gifts God gives us are meant, among other things, to serve others, you'd like students to think of typical situations in their everyday lives where they might use a special ability God has given them to serve others.

Divide students into groups of four. Give each group a sheet of paper and a pen or pencil and ask them to think of typical situations that they experience every day. (For example, school, music practice, Bible study, eating with the family, and so forth.) Once they have thought of a bunch of them, the group should pick one favorite and write it on the sheet of paper.

After they've done that, have each group fold its paper into a paper airplane. (*Note*: You may have to give simple airplane-folding instructions. Some may be paper-airplane-folding impaired. If you are the impaired one, ask a "talented" student to teach you and the group the art of folding one!)

Then have groups divide into two pairs and separate to opposite sides of the room. One pair from each group of four should take the paper airplane with them. Have the pairs who have the airplanes stand on one side of the room and the pairs without airplanes stand on the other. Explain that they are going to fly their airplanes to the pairs across the room, but the pairs catching must catch a different team's airplane. If the airplane doesn't make it all the way to the other side, the throwing pair must pick it up, return to their side and throw it again. Once this is done, have groups of four return and sit together. Each group should now have another team's airplane.

Explain that finding a way to use the gifts that God has given them can feel confusing and be difficult—just like trying to catch a paper airplane. But they must keep searching for the talents God has given them and for a way to use them. Explain: *Now that you have someone else's situation, think about the ways that you could put one of God's gifts into practice in that situation.* Have groups write their ideas on the paper airplanes, then invite them to share the ideas with the whole group.

Close the meeting by having the students pray silently for God's help to use the talents He has given them.

Option 2: Contemplate Your Gifts. You need sheets of paper, pens or pencils and meditative worship music. Suggest that just because God has given us an incredible gift doesn't mean we have immediate knowledge on how to use that gift. But we can commit today to identifying the gifts that God has given us and choosing one way we can use those gifts to serve others.

Have students find a place alone in the room. Play some quiet meditative music and have them contemplate the things they have heard in today's lesson. Then distribute papers and pencils. Have students write "I think my talent is . . ." and "I plan on using it by . . ." on their papers. Then ask them to complete these statements to the best of their ability.

Give them 3 to 5 minutes. When they have completed their statements, have each student find a partner and share their statements with him or her. Instruct the partners to make a verbal commitment to get in touch this week to ask if the other has been able to put his or her talent into practice.

When everyone has had the chance to share, have students sit in a semicircle and place their papers in front of them, face down on the floor. Then ask your adult leadership team to walk around the room, praying for each student individually. When all of the students in the group have received individual prayer, close with a prayer for the whole group.

REFLECT

The following short devotions are for the students to reflect on and answer during the week. You can make a copy of these pages and distribute to your class or print out from the PDF for this session found on *The Life of Jesus* DVD.

1—DON'T KEEP IT TO YOURSELF!

Read 1 Peter 4:10-11 to find out what to do with your gifts.

Lydia had the most beautiful voice and she loved to sing in front of large groups, but she refused to sing in the church choir. "Why should I sing for them?" Lydia replied when her mother asked why she never volunteered for choir. "Someone else will do it; they don't need me."

Tim was really good at playing with little kids. Every day after school he played with his cousins and helped them do their homework. When his dad asked why he didn't volunteer to help tutor kids at his school's Study Buddy program, Tim told him, "I'm just a kid! Besides, it would be hard helping kids I don't know."

God made you with special, built-in talents. But He didn't give them to you just to amuse yourself! He wants you to use them to serve and give to others the way He gave to you.

What is one gift you can use to help a friend today?

_____

_____

_____

_____

2—HOW TO GET STARTED

Dive headfirst into Matthew 7:11. If you're feeling brave, do a cannonball!

If you were making brownies, would you just make up how to do it or would you ask someone for a recipe? If you wanted to fix the brakes on your youth leader's car, would you just do it or would you ask a mechanic to show you how? If you wanted to climb the highest mountain in town, would you just walk outside one day and do it or would you ask someone who'd done it before what to take with you and which path to take?

Do you think God wants you to start serving Him by just doing anything you can without asking Him for help? Or does He want you to ask Him first?

Ask Him to show you how to serve Him by serving one of your family members this week.

3—BEHIND THE SCENES

Find 1 Corinthians 12:18-20 and see what part of the Body you might be.

Daniel was bummed. His brother, Aaron, played guitar for the high school worship band each Sunday. Aaron also helped organize a concert that raised tons of money for a family who lost their house to a fire. He even started a Christian club at his public high school and got straight *As* and was voted vice president of his class. Aaron is so popular that people hardly ever remember Daniel's name. If they even notice him at all, they just call him "Aaron's little brother."

"It's no fair!" Daniel told his pastor. "Aaron's good at so much and I'm only good at setting up the sound system for worship!"

Sometimes it's easy to think that the only jobs worth doing are the ones that get lots of attention. God doesn't think that; He made everyone different with different gifts to serve in lots of different places.

Pray that you'll come to know and use the gifts God gave you.

4—USE IT!

Hey! Read 1 Corinthians 12:1-6 and get clued in!

Rachel, a high school student, plays the piano every week for the children's worship service. Bradley, a retired senior citizen, waters flowers every week in the church parking lot. The senior pastor gives the sermon every Sunday. What do all of these people have in common?

The answer is pretty easy: They are all using the gifts and abilities they have to serve in the church.

Think of two of your friends and figure out what gift(s) they have. How can you encourage them to use their gifts this week?

_____

_____

_____

_____

LIVING OUR FAITH

THE BIG IDEA

Other people need to see us live out the truth.

SESSION AIMS

In this session you will guide students to (1) learn what Jesus says about living out their faith in the world; (2) be motivated to live their faith in their world; and (3) repent of one thing in their lives that keeps them from being Christ's salt and light.

THE BIGGEST VERSE

"You are the salt of the earth. But if the salt loses its saltiness, how can it be made salty again? . . . You are the light of the world. A city on a hill cannot be hidden" (Matthew 5:13-14).

OTHER IMPORTANT VERSES

Ezekiel 16:4; Matthew 5:13-16; 28:16-20; John 1:4; Philippians 2:12-15; James 2:14-17

STARTER

Option 1: Logo Loco. You need a large paper bag, masking tape and several objects bearing a variety of easily recognized logos (such as a hat with the Nike swoosh, a T-shirt with the CK letters for Calvin Klein, a cup with the golden arches from McDonalds, a Pepsi can with the blue and red circle, a pair of surf shorts with the Quiksilver wave, and so on). You will need at least eight different items, preferably with a picture logo, not the company name. You may have to tape over the words on some objects. Make sure logos are ones with which your students are familiar. Ahead of time, place the items in the paper bag to conceal them from the students.

At the meeting, greet students and divide them into two teams. Explain that advertisers work hard to make their products immediately recognizable to the public. Sometimes they use words, sometimes simply a picture to represent their product. You want to see how well the students know their logos—you're going to pull an item out of the bag, and if they know the brand name of the product or company that the logo represents, they should stand up. You will call on the first person to stand. If that person is wrong, the first person from the other team to stand will get to answer.

Pull out the items one by one so that the logo can be clearly seen by both teams. Keep track of which team correctly identifies the company or product and reward the winning team with a round of applause. Follow up by asking the following:

- What are some other logos you can think of that weren't used in the game?
- Have you ever bought a product simply because it had a certain logo? Why?
- What convinced you to buy these products?

Suggest that just as a picture can represent a product—one look and you know who made it—our lives should represent the One who made us. We are God's children and represent Him to the world. When people take a look at us, can they easily identify whom we belong to?

Today you're going to talk about being God's logo—His salt and light—in the world. Our lives should show the world that we belong to Jesus.

Option 2: Commercially Speaking. For this option, you will need 3 to 5 minutes of video footage of TV commercials or infomercials (recorded from TV or from YouTube or a similar online video resource), a way to play the video for everyone, and candy for prizes.

Ahead of time, make up 8 to 10 trivia questions based on what happens in the video clip, such as, "What was the first person in the deodorant commercial wearing?" Be sure to write down the answers for yourself!

At the meeting, greet students and then divide them into two teams (the old standby boys against girls might work here, or maybe you could have adult leaders against students). Ask for three volunteers from each team to be their team's representatives.

Play the video clip, and then ask the trivia questions. When someone knows the answer, she should raise her hand. If she answers correctly, her team gets 1,000 points. If the answer is incorrect, her team loses 1,000 points and the other team gets a chance to answer. If the second team's volunteer doesn't know the answer, the rest of the first team gets to guess.

Once the game is over, give candy prizes to the winning team and discuss:

- What are some of your favorite commercials?
- What makes them your favorites?
- Do you think commercials influence what you buy or maybe what your friends buy?

Explain that the most effective commercials are the ones that show how our lives will be better if we use the product. Then ask students how that selling point is like telling people about Jesus. (The best way to tell people about Jesus is to show that our lives are different. If we are positive, loving and excited about Jesus, then maybe they'll want to try Jesus for themselves. We don't need to "sell" Jesus to others, but we do need to share Jesus, because unlike commercials that claim their products will make your life better, Jesus really will!)

MESSAGE

Option 1: Hit the Lights! You need several Bibles, six or seven objects that would be hard to identify without light, including a jar of *unsalted* peanuts and an identical jar of *salted* peanuts, and a dark bag in which to put the objects.

Ahead of time, think of something on each object for the students to identify. For example, if one of your objects is a book, the students could be asked to read the title, or if one of your objects is an apple, the students could be asked to identify the color. The idea is to ask something that can't be answered without seeing the object in the light. Place the objects in the bag and keep it closed until the game.

At the meeting, divide students into two teams. Call one team "Salt" and the other "Light." Have the teams move to the opposite end of the room from you and sit on the floor in their team groups. Tell them that you are going to have a contest to see which team can correctly identify something about the objects you will pull out of your bag. Explain that they'll need to tell you specifically what you will ask them about the object, whether it's the title, the color, the shape, and so forth

Turn off the lights in the room. Pull the objects out of the bag one by one. If a student thinks he can identify what you're holding, have him stand up and shout out the name of his team. Call on the first person you hear and ask for his answer. If he's correct, say, "That's right!" If he's incorrect, say, "That's wrong!" and don't reveal what the object really is. After the student has guessed, put the object in a place where it can be seen at the end of the game. When all the objects have been used, turn on the lights and let the students see the objects. Hopefully you'll have some funny mistakes to capitalize upon as you ask:

1. What made this game difficult? *It was hard to see without light.*

2. Have you ever searched for something in the dark? *Keys, the door-knob of your house, the name on a street sign, and so forth.*

3. What advantages are there to having light? *We can see clearly.*

Hand out a few unsalted peanuts to each student and instruct them to eat the peanuts. (*Important Note*: Be sure to find out about any peanut allergies!) Next give them the salted peanuts to eat and ask if they can identify the difference between the first and the second peanuts, and ask which they liked more. Isn't it amazing how a few grains of salt can make a big difference in the way something tastes?

Youth Leader Tip

When encouraging your junior-highers to be "salt and light," be sure to lead the way. When you model a lifestyle that goes against the grain of culture, students will be emboldened by your example and more likely to step out and strive to live that way as well.

Transition to the next segment by telling students that Jesus told a story about salt and light. Ask a volunteer to read Matthew 5:13-16, and then explain that Jesus used two images to help us understand what our lives as His followers should be like: *salt* and *light*.[1]

Just as you discovered in your game, things are a lot easier to see when there's light. The same holds true for us as well. People can see the Lord and His great love for them more clearly when we, as His people, live out what we say we believe. Loving, godly lives are like beacons that direct people to Jesus. When we live out our faith in our words and actions, we are being God's representatives and lighting the way for others to find a relationship with Him. When we don't live out our faith in what we do, it's like having a match but never lighting it. Jesus has given us His light; what will we do with it?

Even though our lives may seem small, just like the grains of salt on the peanuts, we can make a big impact on people around us. The "salt" in our lives is what we do to express our faith in God, such as kindness, patience, honesty, and so on. When we live out our faith, others will notice that something is different about us. Then we can tell them why: Jesus has put His Spirit in us and changed us from the inside out!

Option 2: Name That Emotion. You need several Bibles. Ahead of time, ask one of your most outgoing (and maybe even a bit obnoxious) students to prepare to act out the following wrong emotions: She should look very sad but yell, "I'm so happy!" Next, she should look absolutely terrified but moan, "I'm so sad!" Finally, she should act really angry but say, "This is such a terrific day!"

Let students know that today you're going to look at a parable that Jesus told about salt and light. Ask a volunteer to read Matthew 5:13-16. Once he has finished, ask a second student to read it again for emphasis. Then explain that Jesus used the images of salt and light to show that our lives should make a visible or obvious difference in the world around us. Just as we can taste the salt in our food or see the light in a room, we need to live out our faith in a way that makes it obvious who we are: disciples of Jesus. This only happens when we are living out in our actions what we say we believe in our hearts.

Ask the volunteer to come to the front of the room and act out the three scenarios where the emotions don't match the words. Then ask students to identify what didn't make sense about the actor's words. (The action didn't match the words.)

Read James 2:14-17 to the students, then explain that just as it doesn't work when what we say doesn't match how we act, the same is true when we follow

Jesus. If we say we follow Jesus, we should be salt to the bland world around us and a light to our friends who are trying to find the truth. Continue by discussing the following questions:

1. How are we supposed to let our lights shine before others? *By living among people and letting them see Jesus in us.*

2. What are specific ways that you let your light shine? *Opening the door for someone, sharing your lunch, helping someone study, clearing the dinner dishes, volunteering at a day camp, going on a missions trip, and so forth. Any time you touch others with God's love you are shining His light.*

3. What suggestions would you have for someone who feels like he or she can't live out his or her faith? *Remember that the Source of the light is Jesus. With His help we can show others that our faith is real. Being a light is not about proving something; it's about letting the inward change of heart come out naturally in the way you live your everyday life.*

4. Who is the salt that loses its saltiness? *People who say they believe in Jesus but do not live for Him.*

5. What happens when we cover up a light? *It becomes ineffective. People can no longer see their way.*

Read Philippians 2:12-15, emphasizing verse 13, and then ask students how we can be sure that we are being salt and light. (To start with, have a consistent, daily devotional time with the Lord through prayer and reading His Word. Remember, it is God's work in us that enables us to live out our faith in Him.)

DIG

Option 1: Tough Calls. You need a Bible, whiteboard, a dry-erase marker (or chalkboard and chalk) and enough copies of "Tough Calls" (found on the next three pages and on *The Life of Jesus* DVD) for every two students.

Have students form pairs, and then give each pair a copy of "Tough Calls." Ask each pair to prepare a role-play using their assigned situation. Allow a few

TOUGH CALLS

You've been friends with Dylan for about three months. He's been honest with you about everything—including his belief that Christianity is fake and useless. You, on the other hand, have been faithful in attending church and going to youth group all your life.

One day you really blow it. First, Dylan sees you and your mom in a huge argument. Then you get ticked off with another friend and tell him off. You're having a bad day and Dylan takes this opportunity to ask you what the difference is between your beliefs and his. "After all," he says, "you have the same problems I do. Isn't life supposed to be better for you?"

What will you say?
How will you share your faith?

TOUGH CALLS

2

You've been trying to live for Jesus, but sometimes it can be so hard. It's especially difficult to live for Him around your parents. You accepted Christ last summer at camp, but your parents still don't understand what the big deal is. In fact, they have been openly hostile about your faith. But you want to tell them more about Jesus and your desire to live for Him.

It's Friday night, and you're watching television in the den. Your mom comes in and notices that the show you're watching uses some questionable language. Not really *bad* language, but questionable. Just as one actor cuts loose with another creative swearword, you look up and notice your mom frowning at you.

At this moment, you wonder if what you are watching on television is consistent with what you have told your parents about your beliefs.

What will you say?
What will you do?

TOUGH CALLS

You've been dating Betsy for the last six months. You really like her and the two of you have an awesome time together, but you've never spoken with her about your beliefs, and lately you feel like you need to do so.

You've asked Betsy to each lunch with you to have a long talk. She's not sure what to expect, but loves a free lunch and loves being with you. So with Betsy sitting across the table from you, you begin to tell her about your belief in God.

What will you say?
How will you share your faith?

minutes to create the role-plays, encouraging them to be creative as they work through their situations.

After they've created their role-plays, ask for a few pairs to present them in front of the class. After each role-play, ask the audience to suggest other ways to be salt and light.

Once this is done, ask volunteers to share a time when they've tried to tell their friends about Christ, but have felt like failures. Read Matthew 28:16-20 and ask students to brainstorm some ways that they can apply this verse when they feel like they've been rejected for trying to be different from others.

We can know that Jesus is always with us, which empowers us to keep sharing, even if people at first reject our salt and light. Ask students to brainstorm 10 ways they can be like salt and light to people around them this week and write those 10 ideas on the board.

Option 2: True Friendship. You need two copies of "True Friendship" (found on the next page and on *The Life of Jesus* DVD), a white board and a dry-erase marker (or chalkboard and chalk). Ahead of time, choose two of your most self-confident junior high girls to memorize and practice the drama.

At the meeting, have the two girls present the drama. After they have finished, explain that although it seemed like Felicia was on the right track, what Jeannette needed was someone to just listen to her, help her with her homework and come to her birthday party. Telling others about Jesus is important, but sometimes we need to earn the right to be heard first by showing God's love through our words, attitudes and actions.

Ask students to brainstorm some ways that they can earn the right to be heard this week at school. When they have come up with several ideas, ask them how this relates to being salt and light? (Often earning the right to be heard means we have to be bold and different from the people around us, making us salt and light. Felicia would have been a huge light to Jeannette if she

Youth Leader Tip

When you are presenting a story or illustration to your group, it's best if you read it over a couple of times to practice before you present it. It's always a great idea to make the story fresh by telling it as if you have just heard it yourself for the first time.

TRUE FRIENDSHIP

Cast
Jeanette, a non-Christian
Felicia, a Christian

The scene opens with Felicia sitting in a chair, as if at a table in a coffee shop. Jeannette walks in.

Felicia: Hey, Jeannette, what's up?

Jeanette: Hey, Felicia, I haven't seen you in a while. I missed you at my birthday party last week.

Felicia: Yeah, sorry, I just got really busy.

Jeanette: Well, anyway, I'm glad you're here. I'm so upset.

Felicia: Why? What's going on?

Jeannette: Well, since you stopped helping me with math, I've been bombing. I tried to hide my report card from my mom, but she found it in my desk and she is totally ticked. She said that I can't spend more time with friends after school until my grades get better.

Felicia: That stinks.

Jeannette: I know, doesn't it? She's at the grocery store now, so I kinda snuck out. She doesn't know I'm here.

Felicia: (Hesitating) Well, Jeannette, maybe now is a good time to tell you about a Friend of mine.

Jeannette: Yeah, I know, you think that I'm too mean to that new girl Tammy.

Felicia: No, actually, I mean my Friend Jesus. He's my best Friend in the whole world. And even though you can't see any other friends right now, you could ask Him to come into your life and be your Savior.

Jeannette: Look, Felicia, I don't want to hear about Jesus right now. I need someone who is here right now to help me, and here you go telling about some guy who died a long time ago. I need a friend I can see, that I can count on to be there for me! If you were really a friend, you would have come to my birthday party and you would have helped me with my homework.

Jeannette walks off the stage angrily.

had truly befriended her, come to her birthday party and helped her with her homework.) Then ask the students to brainstorm 10 ways they can be good and salty to people around them this week and write those ideas on the board.

APPLY

Option 1: Taking Out the Trash. You need a garbage can with some stinky trash in it, paper and pens or pencils.

Distribute paper and pens or pencils as you explain that living a life that is salt and light to others means we have to get rid of anything that makes our salty flavor bland or dulls our light. Pick up a piece of trash and suggest that anything keeping us from being a light for God is like this piece of trash: stinky and no good.

Ask students to think about one thing in their lives that is blocking their light from others and have them write it down on a piece of paper. When they have finished, ask them to come forward and put their piece of paper in the trash with the rest of the garbage.

When everyone has finished, collect the trash and, if there's a dumpster nearby, walk the entire class to the dumpster and watch all of the things that block their light go into the trash. Close in prayer, asking God to help us continue to remove anything that dulls our ability to be salt and light.

Option 2: Burning the Barriers. You need a container in which to burn paper (such as a large metal trash can or a barbecue), matches, sheets of paper, pens or pencils and a small salt packet for each student (these can be found at a restaurant supply store or your local fast food restaurant). *Caution!* This activity needs to be done outside or you need to take extra precautions to avoid setting off fire alarms or burning down the building!

Explain that God's call to Christians to live a life before non-believing people is a high and holy call. Think about it: We have the opportunity to introduce people to the One who created oceans, capillaries and bugs. And even better, we have the chance to give others the opportunity to live forever. We must not take this opportunity lightly. God's call is also all-consuming. That means that He wants us to get rid of whatever is holding us back from living so that others will see Jesus.

Ask students to think about the way they live. Help them understand that this activity isn't an attempt to push them into changing their lives because of guilt, but a chance to choose to live differently so that others will see God in them. Distribute paper and pens or pencils. Instruct students to write the things on this paper that they need to sacrifice in order to live their lives so that others will see Jesus. (You might need to give them some guidance as to what those things might be.)

When students have finished thinking and writing, light a few papers on fire to get things started. Then invite students to come forward as they feel led and drop their papers in the fire. Instruct them to pray and ask God to help them live a life that is truly salt and light as their papers burn. As students leave, give each one a small salt packet as a reminder to live a "salty" life.

REFLECT

The following short devotions are for the students to reflect on and answer during the week. You can make a copy of these pages and distribute to your class
or print out from the PDF for this session found on *The Life of Jesus* DVD.

1—A MEMBER OF THE CLUB

Jump into 1 Timothy 2:3-4 and see what God wants saved: pennies? Bottle
caps? Gum wrappers?

Did you ever join a club when you were a kid? Did you have to do things like
jump into a river or pull a prank on someone to become a member?

_____

_____

_____

_____

    Does being a Christian mean being in a club where you have to do things
such as dressing right or paying your dues? No! God's gift of salvation is not like
a club membership where only a few get to join. He wants everyone to be
saved! And being saved is not about following rules or paying your dues. It is a
completely new way of living—a total change in heart and lifestyle. When we
let that new life shine through us, others will see the way to God.

What would Jesus say about your life as His follower?

_____

_____

_____

_____

Is there a way to let His light shine even brighter in you this week?

_____

_____

_____

_____

    Pray for God to use you this week to draw someone closer to Himself.

2—BEING BOLD

Feeling bold? Find Acts 5:27-29 and learn what God means by the word "bold."

David felt sort of weird about being a Christian. He went to a public school and took his Bible to school every day, but no one ever gave him a hard time about it. All his non-Christian friends knew that he went to church and none of them stopped being his friend because of it.

One weekend he went to church and the pastor spoke about how important it was to tell your friends about God and to be bold. On Monday, David went to school knowing that it wasn't enough just to take his Bible in his backpack to school with him and let his friends know he went to church. He needed to be bolder and actually tell his friends about Jesus.

David could lose his friends by being more bold. Is it worth it?

If you think so, pray that God will help you be bold with your friends, with your family and with the people you meet each day.

3—GONE FISHIN'

Flip, flip, flip to Matthew 4:19 and find out what complicated things God needs from you!

If you were going fishing, what would you need to take with you?

- ☐ Books about calculus, nuclear physics and pond life
- ☐ A guy named Floyd with a Ph.D. in fishing
- ☐ A fishing pole and some bait
- ☐ A boat made of glass

Fishing is a simple thing that doesn't require lots of fancy stuff. How is that like showing people the truth?

_____

_____

_____

_____

Think about one person with whom you can share the truth with this week.

4—THE BEST FOR LAST

Find Matthew 28:16-20 and see what Jesus saved for last.

Mark went to live with his dad for the summer, on the other side of the country far away from his mom. His mom sent him a long letter after he had been gone only a few days. She told him how his little sister and grandmother were and how things were going with her job. She told him how the weather was and told him a joke she thought he would like.

At the very end of the letter she wrote, "Be good. Make sure you take good care of yourself. Eat good food and sleep enough at night. I love you and miss you." She saved the most important things for last.

Jesus thought that sharing the Good News with everyone was really important. He made it one of the last things He said to us so that we would remember it. Ask God to show you ways to do what He asked all week.

FORGIVENESS

THE BIG IDEA

Forgiveness is always the right choice.

SESSION AIMS

In this session you will guide students to (1) learn that forgiving others makes sense because God forgives us; (2) understand the importance of making forgiving others a daily practice; and (3) commit to choosing one person to forgive, even though it may be tough.

THE BIGGEST VERSE

"Then the master called the servant in. 'You wicked servant,' he said, 'I canceled all that debt of yours because you begged me to. Shouldn't you have had mercy on your fellow servant just as I had on you?'" (Matthew 18:32-33).

OTHER IMPORTANT VERSES

Amos 1:3,6,9,11,13; 2:1,4,6; Matthew 6:14; 18:21-35; Romans 12:18; Ephesians 4:32; Colossians 3:13; 1 Peter 3:9

STARTER

Option 1: Junior's Life. You need one white bedsheet or large piece of white paper, one clear plastic tarp, ketchup, mustard, grape jelly, barbecue sauce and any other colorful liquids (at least five different colors) you can find, paper towels and a trash can or trash bag.

Ahead of time, lay the clear plastic tarp over the white sheet (or paper) on the floor in the center of the room.

At the meeting, welcome students and explain that you're going to start today by taking a look at 24 hours in the life of a typical junior-higher whom we'll call "Junior." Explain that the white bedsheet covered with the plastic tarp represents Junior.

During Junior's day, several interesting things happen. First, he's grumpy in the morning and talks back to his dad. At this point, pour one of the liquids onto the tarp. On his way to school, he makes fun of a kid who falls off his skateboard. Pour a second liquid onto the tarp. Continue naming sins and pouring liquids until you have at least five different liquids poured onto the tarp.

Explain that each of us lives each day similarly to Junior. We do dumb, hurtful or sinful things and make a mess. As you mix up the liquids, tell students that there's only one thing that can clean us up: forgiveness.

Now discuss the following:

1. What does it mean to be forgiven? *It means that whatever we've done wrong is forgotten.*

2. What does the world say forgiveness is? *Forgiving, but not forgetting.*

3. Why is it important that we forgive others? *Because Jesus tells us to. Plus if we don't, we can cause ourselves emotional damage and put a wall between ourselves and others and between ourselves and God.*

4. What does God's forgiveness do? *It washes away our sin and allows us to enter heaven.*

At this point, carefully lift the clear covering with the gross liquids off of Junior as you tell the group that forgiveness is the only thing that can get rid of all the wrong things we do every day. Carefully roll up the tarp and discard it in a trash can or trash bag.

Explain that today you'll be talking about the importance of forgiving others. You'll look at what Jesus says about it and figure out how what He says makes a difference in our own lives.

Option 2: Crime and Punishment. You need newspapers, a large sheet of news-print, large felt-tip markers and masking or transparent tape.

Ahead of time, gather several days' worth of newspapers, especially national newspapers with a wide variety of stories. Read through the newspapers and collect stories about people who have done terrible things such as committing murder, theft or arson and have been convicted in court. Make sure that you have enough of these for each pair of students to have one story. Also ahead of time, tape the large sheet of newsprint to a wall.

As students arrive, welcome them and have them form pairs. Give each pair a news story. Instruct the pairs to read the story and be prepared to report the answers to the following questions:

- What was the crime?
- What was the criminal's attitude?
- What was the punishment?

As groups are preparing their answers, write the three questions on the sheet of paper. When groups are ready, ask them to report their findings to the rest of the class. As they report, write their responses in the appropriate places on the newsprint (or board or overhead).

When all groups have responded, discuss the following:

- What do you notice about punishment?
- What do you notice about the criminals' attitudes?
- If you had been the victim of these crimes, would you be able to forgive these people? How? Why?
- What is the difference between our forgiveness and God's?

Explain that today you'll be talking about the difference between God's forgiveness and ours.

MESSAGE

Option 1: Paper Fight. You need several Bibles, masking tape, a stack of light green paper, rowdy music and a $20 bill that you don't mind giving away. (If $20 is a little steep, $10 or even $5 will also make the point.)

Ahead of time, tape a line down the center of the floor of the meeting room to separate the two teams.

At the meeting, divide students into two teams and explain that they're go-ing to compete in a paper fight. You're going to throw out clumps of green pa-per and students should crumple them up and throw them to the other side of the room. Play a little rowdy music and let the green paper go flying!

Just before you are ready to end the game, take the $20 bill, wad it into a green piece of paper and throw it into the game. End the game and explain that you have a surprise: *There's a $20 (or $10 or $5) bill hidden in one of these pieces of paper and whoever finds it gets to keep it.*

Once someone finds the $20 bill, ask students to imagine that you had only loaned her (or him) the $20 bill instead of giving it to her. Let's say she can't pay it back because she spent all the money on computer games. Since you're a nice person, you decide to let her off the hook. But the next day, she sees someone in the hallway at school who owes her a quarter, and she asks him for it. He says that he can't give it to her today, but maybe sometime next month. She is so angry that she yells at him in front of his friends. Do the students think this is fair? Why or why not?

Explain that Jesus told a similar story in Matthew 18:21-35.[1] Ask for a vol-unteer to read the passage aloud, then discuss:

1. Who does the king represent? *God.*

2. Who does the servant represent? *Us.*

3. What is the significance of the difference in the size of the debts? *The larger debt is our sin; the smaller debt is what others owe us.*

4. What is the significance of the king canceling the servant's debt? *This is a demonstration of God's forgiveness.*

5. Why did the servant treat his fellow servant harshly? *Because the ser-vant didn't understand forgiveness and was taking the king's forgive-ness for granted.*

Youth Leader Tip

Remember that games like the one above can can easily get out of hand. Be on the lookout for students that are being too rough or who aren't playing fairly. Sometimes the rowdiest in the group will be the adult volunteers, so be sure to remind them to keep it a bit mellow.

6. What does Jesus want us to learn from this parable? *Jesus wants us to forgive others in the same way that we've been forgiven. He wants us to understand that our debt to Him is far greater than anyone's debt to us, yet He forgives us completely!*

Explain that while we all might have different perspectives on what Jesus said, the truth is that He has called us to forgive others. It doesn't matter what others have done to us; forgiveness is always the right thing to do.

Option 2: Forgiveness Perspectives. You need several Bibles, two adult volunteers, one copy of "Forgiveness Perspectives" (found on the following three pages and on *The Life of Jesus* DVD), paper and pens or pencils.

Ahead of time, ask one of the adult volunteers to come to you at the start of class and tell you in front of the students, "Hey, I know you owe me $20, but don't worry about it. Just call it a gift from me." Ask the other adult to play along with you when you belligerently ask him for the dollar that he owes you so that you can go get a soda.

At the meeting, cue the first adult volunteer to mention your $20 debt. Begin telling a story about something that happened to you this week, then say to the second adult volunteer, "I am so thirsty. Remember, you owe me a dollar? Can I have it now so I can go get a soda right after the meeting?" At this point the adult who allegedly owes you a dollar should explain that she didn't have time to go to the bank, so she's going to have to pay you later. You should get really mad at her—if you think you can pull it off, storm out of the room saying something like, "Fine, I'll just figure out how to get a drink myself!"

This will undoubtedly freak out students—which is exactly what you want to do. The surprise will make this step all the more memorable and powerful. Come back into the room and ask students what they were thinking as you got angry at the adult who owed you one dollar. Comment on how ironic and ludicrous this is since you were just forgiven a debt of $20.

Explain that Jesus told a similar story; then ask a volunteer to read Matthew 18:21-35 aloud. Discuss the following questions:

1. What are some of the similarities between what happened today and this story that Jesus tells?

2. Who does the king represent? *God.*

3. Who does the servant represent? *Us.*

FORGIVENESS PERSPECTIVES

Take a journey through time and imagine that
you're this person, living in Jesus' time.

You're a Jewish person. Your father, your father's
father and your father's father's father have believed in God
and have left you with the wonderful heritage and history
of Israel. All that heritage has caused you to trust in God
as a righteous Judge. You believe that God loves
all people, but that when someone sins against Him,
he or she deserves His wrath. Therefore you believe
that once someone wrongs you more than three times,
you should not forgive him or her. News has just
reached you about what Jesus says about forgiveness.

What are your reactions?

FORGIVENESS PERSPECTIVES

Take a journey through time and imagine that
you're this person, living in Jesus' time.

You're a murderer on the run. Last year in a fit of
passion and rage, you killed a man for stealing the grain out of your
storage shed. You aren't proud of what you did, but the grain
that the man stole was supposed to feed your family and has
left your kids without food. You aren't familiar with Jewish teachings,
but you do know that murder is a pretty big deal. And because
you don't want to get caught, you've uprooted your family,
sold your home and have been on the move for the past
six months. News has just reached you about what
Jesus says about forgiveness.

What are your reactions?

FORGIVENESS PERSPECTIVES

Take a journey through time and imagine that
you're this person, living in Jesus' time.

_____

You're a Gentile. At least that's what people call you—
you really have no idea what you are, but you do know that
your family history has been less than religious. Hey, you're
not the most evil person in the world. You have broken a few of the
laws that the Jews talk about, but it's not like you've murdered
anyone. And you've never stolen either (unless that candy bar
from the synagogue fundraiser last year counts). You believe
that God is real, but you haven't worked too hard at
understanding His teachings. News has just reached you
about what Jesus says about forgiveness.

What are your reactions?

4. What is the significance between the difference in the size of the debts? *The larger the debt of our sin, the smaller the debt of what others owe us.*

5. What is the significance of the king canceling the servant's debt? *Jesus is showing us an awesome picture of His forgiveness.*

6. Why does the servant treat his fellow servant harshly? *Because he doesn't understand what forgiveness is and because he is greedy.*

7. What does Jesus want us to learn from this parable? *Forgiving others is something we must do. We must forgive others in the same way we've been forgiven. Jesus wants us to understand that our debt to Him is far greater than anyone's debt to us, yet He forgives us completely!*

Explain that Jesus communicated the importance of forgiveness to His listeners. He pointed out that since we've been forgiven so much, we should forgive others. Help students understand that in Jewish law, forgiving others three times was normal, but Jesus makes the point that we are supposed to constantly forgive others. Jesus' use of "seventy times seven" was tongue-in-cheek. He doesn't want us just to multiply those numbers (490, by the way) and only forgive someone that many times; He wants us to see that we need to forgive an indefinite number of times.

Divide students into three groups. Give each group one of the "Forgiveness Perspectives" cards. Instruct them to read their assigned perspective and answer the questions from that perspective. Allow groups five minutes to read the passage and write their answers. When groups are finished, have them share their reactions with the whole group.

DIG

Option 1: Jim Gets Clubbed. You need several Bibles and the story below.

Gather the students in the center of the room, and then read the following story to them:

Jim always wanted a job at the fitness club. Ever since he could remember, working at the club was what he hoped to do when he turned 16. He loved working out. He loved talking about working out. He loved playing racquetball and swimming with his friends at the club. Through the years, he'd maintained a great friendship with the owner. Often when things were slow at the club, he and the owner, Bob, would see who could bench press the most. Jim would always lose, but he didn't care. Just being with Bob made it worthwhile. Bob had promised to hire Jim when he was old enough.

Every birthday was one year closer to his dream. Every year Jim looked forward to the day when Bob would hire him. Jim didn't want to run the place. He didn't even want to move up in the fitness world. He just wanted to work at the club. It meant everything to him.

Jim was ecstatic when his sixteenth birthday came. His parents got him an old used car. "Great!" Jim thought to himself, "I can use this to get back and forth from the club. And the money I make there will certainly be enough to pay for the gas!"

His birthday was on a Sunday and the club was closed. So on Monday he went down after school to talk to Bob about the job he had promised Jim. Jim bounced into Bob's office singing "Happy Birthday" as a little hint of why he was there.

"Hi, Jim. What's up?"

"*Well*, I'm 16 now. And you promised me that when I turned 16 you would hire me. So here I am! When do I start?"

"Oh! Well, you see, Jim, it's like this. I like hanging out with you. You're a great kid. But I don't think you've got what it takes to work here. I really don't need anyone to work afternoons and evenings. And all my talk about giving you a job? I was just kidding with you. I thought you understood."

Jim flew into a rage. He shoved Bob and slammed the office door. And as he stomped to his car, he said some things that he wished he hadn't. And now, even though working at the club was what he had always wanted, it was the last place he ever wanted to be.

Next, discuss the following questions:

- What did Bob do wrong?
- Was Jim's reaction appropriate?
- Should Jim forgive Bob? Why or why not?
- Should Bob forgive Jim for losing control?
- Why is forgiving others so difficult?
- What is the best way for us to handle ourselves when we need to forgive someone?

(If students have a hard time coming up with constructive answers to the last, suggest that they should: Take time to think. Ask for reasons why the hurt happened. Seek out someone you can trust to talk to about your hurt.)

Divide students into four groups. Assign each group one of the following verses: Matthew 6:14; Ephesians 4:32; Colossians 3:13; 1 Peter 2:9. Have groups read their assigned verse, then have group members share with each other about a time when they had difficulty forgiving someone and how their assigned verse relates to their need to forgive others.

Wrap up by explaining that God reminds us of His forgiveness so that we'll mirror His actions. Even though forgiving others feels like it might be impossible, His grace and strength can help us do it.

Option 2: Forgiveness Testimonies. You need several Bibles and an adult volunteer. Ahead of time, ask one of the adult volunteers, a student or someone else in your church to come prepared to give a brief testimony about a specific way someone has hurt them and how they are learning—or have already learned—to forgive that person. Ask the person sharing the testimony to share authentically and vulnerably about the pain he or she has experienced, how difficult it can be to forgive someone and how freeing it is to forgive. (Warn the volunteer to be careful not to use names or details that would give hints to the identity of the forgiven person.)

At the meeting, point out that forgiving others can be a very hard thing to do. Let students know that you've invited someone to tell about how he (or she) has been learning about forgiveness firsthand. Invite the person you've prepared in advance to give his or her testimony. Then discuss the following with the whole group:

1. Why is forgiving others so difficult? *Because we are human and feel things deeply. When we're wronged, it takes a lot of work to forgive.*

Youth Leader Tip

When working with junior-highers, the rule is to always expect the unexpected. Not every discussion will go the way that you planned, so always be willing to leave the lesson for a bit (or trash it altogether) for the sake of going to where the students need you to go.

2. What happens if we choose not to forgive people? *Ultimately, we aren't doing what Jesus asks us to do.*

3. Is there anything someone can to do to us that is not forgivable? *Nope, especially when we remember all the "stuff" God forgives us for!*

Explain that God reminds us of His forgiveness so that we'll mirror His actions. God wants us to forgive like He does. Read Ephesians 4:32 and 1 Peter 3:9 to help students understand this fact.

Help students also understand that God commands us to forgive everyone who wrongs us. We should always hope that others will ask for our forgiveness, but God says that we should forgive even if that's not the case. He asks us to forgive no matter what, who, when or where.

APPLY

Option 1: Forgiveness Certificate. You need enough copies of "Forgiveness Certificate" (found on the next page and *The Life of Jesus* DVD) for everyone, and pens or pencils.

Explain that God's call on our lives to forgive people is a lifestyle call. God isn't asking us to just forgive a few people; rather, He is asking us to make forgiveness part of who we are. Sometimes that can be very difficult. Tell students that you will give them an opportunity to make a commitment to choose to live a life of forgiveness.

Distribute the "Forgiveness Certificate" to the group and hand out the pens or pencils. As students are completing the handouts, instruct them to take a moment to look at the certificate and consider what they are doing. They are telling God that they are willing to forgive people who wrong them no matter what, when or why.

Request students to leave their certificates with you when they leave, letting them know that you'll mail them later to remind them of their commitments. (*Note:* To save time, give the envelopes to students and ask them to address envelopes to themselves before leaving.) Be sure to mail students' certificates 30 days after this study to serve as a reminder of the commitments they've made.

Option 2: Tape It to the Cross. You need 3x5-inch index cards, pens or pencils, transparent tape and a cross—either a large wooden one, a cardboard cutout or one drawn on a large sheet of paper and taped to the wall.

Forgiveness Certificate

I hereby promise to live a life of righteousness. I plan on making it a daily practice to tell others that I forgive them. I also promise not to hold a grudge against someone who has done something wrong to me.

_____ Signature

_____ Date

_____ Witness

"Bear with each other and forgive whatever grievances you may have against one another. Forgive as the Lord forgave you" (Colossians 3:13).

Begin by explaining that God's desire for us to forgive people is essential for a number of reasons. First, we must forgive people because He asks us to. Second, we must forgive people because it's the best way to have relationships with others. And finally, God wants us to forgive people because He knows that if we don't, it might cause us permanent emotional pain, which leads eventually to bitterness.

Ask students to close their eyes. Point out that we have all been wronged by someone, and you would like them to think about someone who did something to them that they might not have forgiven yet. If they need to forgive someone, now is the time to ask God for help in taking the first step.

Distribute index cards and pens or pencils. Instruct students to write something that has happened to them that's hard to forgive. To ensure confidentiality, suggest that students write only the first letter of whatever happened to them, such as writing G for "gossiping about me" or L for "lying about me."

Allow two or three minutes for writing, then explain that the best way to ask God for help is to lay our burdens at the Cross. When we do that, we are saying that we know we can't do it on our own, but we need Him to help us. Invite students to tape their cards to the cross.

When everyone has taped their cards, have students gather in a circle around the cross and close with prayer, asking God for help in forgiving others.

After students leave, be sure to completely destroy their notes to ensure confidentiality.

REFLECT

The following short devotions are for the students to reflect on and answer during the week. You can make a copy of these pages and distribute to your class or print out from the PDF for this session found on *The Life of Jesus* DVD.

1—HOW MANY TIMES?

Don't go anywhere until you've read Matthew 18:21-22 and done a little math!

Andrew was *so* fed up with his little sister. While he was at school, she had gone into his room and into his drawers. She took a black marker and wrote all over the pages of his math book and she let his lizard, Elvis, out of his cage. This wasn't the first time either. She did things like that all the time! Only yesterday she used his brand-new toothbrush to do her Barbie's hair.

When she came to apologize, Andrew said, "I have forgiven you a zillion times. I don't have to forgive you anymore!"

Is that true?

Jesus wasn't giving us a specific number when He told the disciples to forgive "seventy time seven." He wants us to keep on forgiving and forgiving and forgiving, even when it seems like we've done it a million times.

Ask God to help you forgive anyone who hurts you this week.

2—FORGIVENESS IS HARD

Discover Luke 11:2-4 and read an oldie but goodie.

How many times have you heard The Lord's Prayer? One million times? Or maybe just twice? Are the things in it easy to do? Is it easy to forgive the most popular person in school if she does something mean to you? What about the least popular? What about your siblings or your mom and dad?

How easy is it to forgive all the time? Do you think God tells us to do these things because they are easy? Explain.

_____

_____

_____

_____

Why does Jesus think forgiveness is so important?

_____

_____

_____

_____

3—MISSING THE POINT

Flip to Luke 6:37-38, and then you be the judge of whether or not you should be the judge.

Gina had more Bible awards than anyone had ever seen. She had 44 blue ribbons for memorizing Bible verses in elementary school, she had a pile of award Bibles that she never opened collecting dust in the corner of her closet, and she had two big gold trophies for winning the National Bible Verse Competition two years in a row. In spite of all these awards for knowing so much of the Bible, Gina was mean to others and acted like she was a better Christian than anyone who had lived before.

Do you ever act like Gina? Pray that God will get His Word from your ears to your brain and into your heart, helping you love and forgive everyone—just like God loves and forgives you!

4—HOW HARD IS IT TO FORGIVE?

See if you can find Colossians 3:13-14 in under 15 seconds!
How hard would it be to forgive . . .

- The most popular girl in school if she bumped into you and caused you to drop all your books and papers right in front of all her friends who laughed at you?

- Your sister who ate the pizza you were saving for your snack after school when you were starved?

- The least popular guy in school if he spilled a milkshake on you just before you had to give an oral report in English?

Is it easier to practice forgiveness once in a while or every day? Who is the one person who has hurt you in the past that you should forgive?

SERVICE

THE BIG IDEA

Helping someone else is like helping Jesus.

SESSION AIMS

In this session you will guide students to (1) realize that serving others is like serving Jesus; (2) be encouraged to serve others even when the going gets tough; and (3) choose one specific way they can serve their friends or family this week.

THE BIGGEST VERSE

"For I was hungry and you gave me something to eat, I was thirsty and you gave me something to drink, I was a stranger and you invited me in, I needed clothes and you clothed me, I was sick and you looked after me, I was in prison and you came to visit me" (Matthew 25:35-36).

OTHER IMPORTANT VERSES

Matthew 10:40-42; 25:31-46; John 3:16; 14:6; Ephesians 2:8-9; James 2:14-16; 1 Peter 4:11; 1 John 1:12-15

STARTER

Option 1: Work Bull's-Eye. You need five Ping-Pong balls, a large sheet of paper, felt-tip pens, masking tape and a bag of candy.

Ahead of time, draw a huge bull's-eye of four concentric circles on the large sheet of paper. Label the outside circle "Easy Work," the next circle "Medium Work," the third circle "Hard Work" and the inside circle "Mega-Hard Work." Tape the paper on the wall at the front of the meeting room. Wrap Ping-Pong balls with the masking tape with the sticky side out.

At the meeting, greet students warmly and then ask for five volunteers. Explain that you're going to ask the volunteers to toss one of the Ping-Pong balls at the bull's-eye. When the ball lands in one of the circles, the group must choose a corresponding task for the student who threw the ball. For example, if a ball lands in the "Medium Work" area, the group might suggest a job like combing the hair of someone in the audience. Or if a ball lands in the "Hard Work" area, the group might suggest rearranging the room. (*Note*: Make sure that students suggest tasks that are appropriate both in terms of level of difficulty and in terms of how much time you have.)

Once a volunteer has received an assignment, have him or her stand aside and wait for the other volunteers to complete their toss. When every volunteer has tossed a ball and received an assignment, explain that they must work fast to complete their assignments. Give them the signal to begin. As volunteers are working, encourage the rest of the class to cheer them on. Reward the volunteers with the candy. When students are finished, congratulate them on their efforts, and then discuss the following:

- How does having different responsibilities feel?
- Were your jobs fair?
- What's the difference between easy service and hard service?
- Is everyone called to do the same type of service? Why or why not?
- Why should we help others?

Transition to the next step by explaining that today, you'll be discussing *why* we should serve as well as *how* we should do it.

Option 2: Pressure Stories. You need several copies of "Pressure Stories" (found on the next page and on *The Life of Jesus* DVD).

Ahead of time, cut the four individual "Pressure Stories" apart so that you can give one to each student in each of the four groups.

PRESSURE STORIES

Phil and Bill want to mow lawns in their neighborhood but are having difficulty in finding people who will let them mow with a pair of scissors and hedge clippers.

Brenda really wants to serve in an orphanage in Mexico with some friends from her junior high ministry. When she arrives at the Mexico City airport, she finds out there's no translator. Her Spanish is good enough to order a taco or burrito, but that's about it.

John wants to go to the deepest part of Africa to serve the people there. But he's discouraged when his youth pastor tells him that they won't be moved by his operatic rendition of Handel's Messiah as a witnessing tool.

Amelia is convinced that she can serve others by using her gift of painting. But she's upset to learn that the church board won't let her paint a life-size picture of Noah's Ark on the side of the church.

At the meeting, greet students and divide them into four equal groups. Explain that you're going to give each group a card with a situation on it. Tell that you'd like everyone to remain totally silent as they read their story.

When everyone has read their group's story, each group will come forward one at a time to tell their assigned story in their own words and give a possible ending for the story. There is one more thing: *Each person may share only seven words per turn!* For example, if their story is about someone who wants to serve by washing cars, it might go something like, "Bill wanted to serve others by washing . . ." and then the next person might say, ". . . cars, so he headed out to get . . ." and the next person would continue. The story can't end until every student from the group has gone twice. Give groups a few minutes to decide their ending; then have them tell their story.

When groups are finished presenting, discuss the following:

- What's the best way to serve others when we aren't sure how to do it?
- What should we do when serving others is difficult?
- Should we quit serving when we feel like it's too difficult?

Explain that sometimes serving others can feel like we're attempting a difficult task, but you're going to see today that God calls us to serve even when it gets tough or is not appreciated.

MESSAGE

Option 1: TP Sculpture. You need several Bibles, a long table, six rolls of toilet paper, a bucket of water, six plastic or paper cups and six pieces of cardboard (or paper plates).

Ahead of time, write out the following sets of Scripture passages from Matthew 25, each on a separate piece of paper: 31-34; 35-36; 37-38; 39-40; 41-43; 44-46.

Youth Leader Tip

Service can sound like a four-letter word to students. To get them to drop their TV remotes or stop text-messaging for a few minutes to get out and serve, try offering them a variety of different service projects. Ask other adult volunteers to help you in leading these projects.

At the meeting have students get into six groups and assign each group one of the Scripture passages. Give each group a piece of cardboard (or paper plate), a roll of toilet paper and a plastic or paper cup. Have them fill the cup with water from the bucket.

Explain that each group is to read the passage that they've been assigned, then brainstorm ways they could make that passage into a sculpture using the toilet paper and water. When the groups are finished, display their creations in scriptural order on the table at the front of the room. Once the sculptures are arranged in order, begin reading the passage. When you come to the end of an assigned section, have the group for that section present their sculpture.

When the groups have finished reading their sections and presenting their sculptures, ask:

1. Who is the Son of Man? *Jesus.*
2. What does "he will separate the sheep from the goats" mean? *It means that He will judge us.*
3. Why are the sheep allowed to enter heaven and the goats aren't? *Because the sheep did what Jesus asked.*
4. Who do the righteous represent? *People who do what God asked.*
5. Who does the king represent? *God.*
6. Why did Jesus tell His disciples this parable? *Jesus wanted them to understand the importance He places on serving the people that society has forgotten.*

Help students realize that the disciples wanted to have the title of "disciple," but preferred not to work hard for it. Jesus wants part of our job description to read "take care of people that others have forgotten." Continue by asking the following questions:

1. How is it possible to serve people the way Jesus wants us to? *We need to rely on God's power.*

2. If you ask Jesus to take over your life but then don't serve, will you still go to heaven? *Yes, you will go to heaven, but you won't experience the true joy of following and serving Him here on earth.*

Explain that Jesus wants us to see that when we serve people who are in need or destitute, we are really serving Him. It's important that we adopt this attitude in our lives. We can't just serve people one day a year and think that's enough. Jesus wants us to make serving Him by serving others a key part of our lives as His followers. Now discuss the following:

- How are we supposed to make this part of our lives?
- How easy is it to do what Jesus says?
- Can everyone serve in the way Jesus is asking?

Explain to students that next you're going to explore how to make serving a reality in our lives.

Option 2: Job Description. You need several Bibles, paper and pens or pencils.

Distribute the paper and pens or pencils and explain that you want students to think about what the job description might be for a Christian. Every job they'll have in life will have some sort of description, so why not think about what a Christian's job description would be? Tell students to find a partner and together write a job description for a Christian. (*Note*: If your students are not familiar with job descriptions, bring yours as an example to get them started.)

When pairs are finished, have them share their descriptions with the rest of the class; then discuss:

- What things did you leave off your descriptions that others included?
- Did any of you put "serving others" on your descriptions?
- How important is serving others to our lives as believers?

Distribute Bibles and have students open to Matthew 25:31-46. Ask them to follow along with you as you read. When you're finished reading, discuss:

1. Who is the Son of Man? *Jesus.*
2. What does "he will separate the sheep from the goats" mean? *It means that He will judge us.*
3. Why are the sheep allowed to enter heaven and the goats aren't? *Because the sheep did what Jesus asked.*
4. Who do the righteous represent? *People who do what God asked.*
5. Who does the king represent? *God.*
6. Why did Jesus tell His disciples this parable? *He wanted them to understand the importance He places on serving the people that society has forgotten.*

Help students realize that the disciples wanted to have the title of "disciple," but preferred not to work hard for it. Jesus has told us that a Christian's job description is to "take care of people that others have forgotten."

DIG

Option 1: Something to Drink. You need one paper cup of water for each student. Before you begin the discussion, make sure that each student has a cup of water. It might be easier for you to give each student an empty cup and begin this step at a water fountain (or have pitchers of cold water available).

Instruct students not to drink the water. Explain that you're all going to go for a short walk. When Jesus asks us to help people, it's like giving us a cup of water and saying, "Someone is thirsty; go find that person and give him or her something to drink." Lead students to your church's sanctuary (If a service is in progress, don't go in!) and ask:

- What types of thirsty people might be here?
- Are these the types of people Jesus might want us to help?
- How might we help these people?

Stop next at the front door of your church. Explain to students that people come to church for a variety of reasons, and then ask:

- Why do people come to this church?
- Are these the types of people Jesus wants us to help?
- How might we help these people?

Lead students outside to a sidewalk, and then ask:

- What types of people pass our church every day?
- Are these the people Jesus wants us to help?
- How might we help them?

Lead students back to the meeting room, and then ask:

- Who passes through this room?
- Which of your friends is Jesus calling you to help?
- How might you help them?

Ask students to look at their cups of water. Explain that their cups of water represent both spiritual and physical help. Ask them to think about people they have contact with who might need these things. It might be someone they notice on the street or it might be someone they know very well. Either way, Jesus calls us to serve. Who do they need to serve?

Read Matthew 10:40-42 and discuss what this passage says about serving others. Have students trade their cups of water with another person in the group and then drink the water.

Option 2: Damsel in Distress. You need a female friend to help you.

Ahead of time, arrange for your friend to rush into the room and interrupt the class, saying, "Hey, I'm sorry to bug you, but I've got a bunch of boxes to unload and I don't know what to do. Can you please come help me?"

At the meeting, reemphasize that we can't just serve people one day a year and think that's enough; Jesus wants us to make serving Him by serving others a key part of our lives as His followers. Focus on this teaching point as your friend comes in and interrupts class. Make sure you clearly tell your friend that you can't help her right now. See how the students respond as you keep talking about the importance of service. After the exchange, discuss:

- Do you think I should have helped that woman?
- Why or why not?
- Did any of you want to get up and help even though I said we were busy?

If any students did try to go help, affirm those students for their servant attitude. Read James 2:14-16 and explain that God is calling us to serve others all the time. What He's looking for is an attitude of service. He wants us to be mindful of people who need to be served. If we can learn to notice people who are needy, we'll not just notice the need, we'll also be able to do more than just give lip service to a need—we'll actually do something to meet it.

APPLY

Option 1: Service in Action. You need plenty of time to do this step and an adult volunteer for every 6 to 10 students. Ahead of time, brainstorm with the adult volunteers to come up with some service ideas to use as suggestions if needed during this step.

Have students form groups of 6 to 10 people, making sure that students who don't know many others join a group (or maybe form their own group). Explain that we can use service as a way to help our friends see the gospel in action! Right now each group is going to plan something that they can do to serve someone else. Whatever they plan, it should be something that their unchurched friends can help with too, so that they can see that Christians do more than just sit around—they act, too!

Have the adult volunteers each join a group and instruct the group to plan a service opportunity that will involve everyone in their group. Students will need to organize it and pull it off, and the adult will serve as a consultant. Your responsibility will be to find out what they have planned and when they plan to do it, as well as to offer encouragement to invite their friends to serve too. If your schedule allows, you might even want to go help them.

When the groups have finished planning, have them present their ideas. Read 1 John 3:14-15 and close the meeting with a prayer asking God to use their service as a message about following Christ. In the next week or two, allow groups to share what they did and what the results were.

Option 2: Committed to Serve. You need your Bible. Instruct the group to sit in a circle. As you look at each of them, explain that you'd like each of them to commit to serving people. Ask everyone to shut their eyes and then silently let God know how they feel about committing to a life of serving Him.

After about 30 seconds, tell students to keep their eyes shut and explain that if they're ready to live a life that totally serves God, you want them to stand. If they just don't feel ready, have them stay seated. And if they aren't sure but might be willing, have them get on their knees.

Let them know how proud you are of their commitments. Reaffirm that serving Jesus by serving others is a call to sacrifice our lives. God calls us to give our all when we serve. With students' eyes still closed, read 1 Peter 4:11, then close the meeting by asking God to help them love others by serving them.

Youth Leader Tip

Even junior-highers lead busy lives. To get them interested in service projects, plan ones that are short. Cut the fluff, pick them up, help them serve, and then take them home. Also, be sure to show them the impact of their service, as this will encourage them to do more.

REFLECT

The following short devotions are for the students to reflect on and answer during the week. You can make a copy of these pages and distribute to your class or print out from the PDF for this session found on *The Life of Jesus* DVD.

1—FREE DAY

To find out what to do with your freedom, read Galatians 5:13-14.

If you had a whole day to do anything you wanted, what would you do?

- ❑ Eat pizza, watch TV and talk on the phone.
- ❑ Go shopping and out to the movies.
- ❑ Help out at a soup kitchen washing dishes.
- ❑ Eat sugar out of the bag with a spoon and drink chocolate syrup like it was water.

What would Jesus want you to do with your free day?

_____

_____

_____

_____

_____

How is it different from what you might want to do?

_____

_____

_____

_____

_____

How can you make your own wants and Jesus' wants come together?

_____

_____

_____

_____

_____

2— NO THANK-YOUS

Hurry to Ephesians 6:7-8 and read it carefully!

Cori was so tired she felt sick. She hadn't really wanted to go to Mexico that weekend but she felt she had to. *After all*, she thought, *God says that I have to serve others.*

All weekend long, she waited for the kids to say thank you for doing a craft with them, but all they said was, "More crafts!" She waited for the family that her church group was building the house for to say thank you, but they didn't say anything.

Cori felt cheated and mad. Didn't these people understand she had better things to do than go to Mexico and build houses for people who didn't care?

God never tells you to be a servant because really great things will happen to you and the people you serve will always be grateful. He wants us to serve others because He first served us.

Pray that God would give you a heart that wants to help others.

3—SELECTIVE SERVICE

Jump into 1 Timothy 6:1-2 and see what you find!

Who are you the most careful to be a "good Christian servant" around?

- ❑ Your Christian friends
- ❑ The Christian family who lives down the street
- ❑ Your non-Christian teacher
- ❑ Your own family

Do you sometimes get sloppy when you are living out your Christianity around other Christians? Do you ever forget to serve at church or to help your Christian friends?

What is one way you can serve in your church this month?

_____

_____

_____

_____

_____

4—USE YOUR GIFTS

Run as fast as you can to 2 Corinthians 9:12-15 to find out what can happen when you give with all your heart.

Maggie is great with kids, so she volunteers in the nursery on Saturday nights. James is great in math, so he helps tutor fourth graders. Liesel is really dependable, so she makes sure all the lights are turned off in the youth group room after everyone leaves on Sundays. Max is pretty good on the drums, so he plays in the worship band.

God wants us to serve Him using the talents He gave us! Everyone has some way he or she can serve his or her church and every way is important.

Pray that God will help you find a special way to serve Him and other believers today.

HOW TO
UNDERSTAND
THE BIBLE

THE MOST POPULAR
BOOK IN THE WORLD

Which book is found in more homes in America than any other book?

Which book is translated into more languages than any other book?

Which book has sold more copies in Europe than any other book?

Do you have the answers to these questions? Well, it's a bit of a trick, be-cause the answer to all three questions is the same. You guessed it . . . the Bible. The Bible is the most popular book in all history and is the most widely read and translated book throughout the world.

Lots of people own Bibles and have them sitting on their dressers or book-shelves. But the tragedy is that that's all they're doing—sitting there, hardly ever opened, just getting dusty.

You can't understand the Bible by letting it sit on the shelf, and putting it under your pillow while you sleep won't work either. If you want to understand the Bible, the most popular book in the world, you have to get three things.

I. Get the Plan

Lots of times we don't read the Bible because we don't know where to start. Af-ter all, it's really big—66 books in one—written by 40 authors over a period of

1,600 years and written in three different languages: Hebrew, Greek and Aramaic. With all of that staring you in the face, how do you know where to start?

That's why you need a plan. You might choose to read just one chapter a day, or maybe even three or four chapters a day to finish the Bible in one year. You might read the books in the order they come in—starting at Genesis and ending in Revelation—or maybe read what you're learning in church. The important thing is to come up with a plan that works for you and lets you study the different parts of the Bible so that you understand it.

2. Get the Point

Read the text you've planned and ask yourself this important question: *What does the passage mean?* When people read the Bible and don't ask that question, they come up with some funky ideas. Try three things to help you figure out what a passage means. First, make sure you get a Bible that has words you can understand. There are many translations; ask your youth leader or pastor for help in choosing one. Second, make sure you read the footnotes or margin notes to help you figure out the meaning of the passage. Third, ask the Holy Spirit to help you understand what you read.

Imagine telling a friend to do something really important, and the next thing you know, he's gone off skateboarding and totally forgotten what you asked him to do. That's what happens every time we read the Bible and don't do what God says. To stop that from happening, ask yourself a second question: *What does this passage mean to me? How does what it says relate to my family, friends, school, church, friends who don't know Jesus, next-door neighbors, and even the guy I talk to at the donut shop?* Every time you read, come up with one specific way to apply what the Bible says to your own life.

3. Get the Team

Most things in life are easier if you do them with someone else. The same is true with understanding the Bible. Pick one friend and ask him or her to be on your team and help you keep on track. Have a five-minute phone conversation with him or her every week to share what you're learning. Or ask him or her to email you to see if you've read the Bible today. Just knowing that someone will ask you what Scripture you're on and what you're learning will help you keep on track.

The bottom line: Spend a few minutes a day and make the Bible the most popular book in your life, too.

ENDNOTES

Session 1: Dead Man Walking
1. The schedule of events in John 11 might look something like this: (1) on day one, the messenger comes to Jesus, and Lazarus dies; (2) on day two, the messenger returns to Bethany; (3) on day three, Jesus waits another day, and then departs; (4) on day four, Jesus arrives at Bethany and raises Lazarus from the dead.

Session 2: The Main Thing
1. The sanctity of the seventh day of the week was a distinctive part of the faith of the Jewish community. God had made it a symbol of the covenant between Himself and His people (see Exodus 20:8-11; 31:12-17). Some rabbis even taught that the Messiah could not come until Israel had perfectly kept the Sabbath. This made obeying the laws of the Sabbath very important to the Jews both personally and nationally.

Session 3: The Biggest One
1. We learn something else interesting in John 20:4: Peter and John were running. The only other passage in the New Testament that refers to actual running (and not to running as a metaphor) is Matthew 28:8, which describes how the women ran to tell the disciples the news of Jesus' resurrection. Running reveals the powerful emotions that drove the disciples forward. In this case, Peter, who was probably older than John, reached the tomb after John.

Session 4: Believe It or Not
1. Jesus also told her in Mark 5:34 to "go in peace." When He said these words to her, He was using a common Jewish farewell, but He was also saying something much more—to go as someone who had been restored and reconciled to her God. Her healing wasn't just physical; it was also spiritual.

Session 5: Do You Want It?
1. Notice that in many Bibles, John 5:4 is absent or sometimes added as a footnote (as in the *New International Version*, for instance). The reason for this is because the verse does not appear in manuscripts dated prior to the fourth century. We don't know for sure where this pool was located, but it was possibly located in the northwest corner of Jerusalem. The theory is that verse four was added later to explain why the water sometimes moved—a sign that the water would heal the afflicted. This might be one of those rare times in the Bible where a detail was added at a later point in history.
2. Adapted from Jim Burns, general editor, *Uncommon Games and Icebreakers* (Ventura, CA: Gospel Light, 2008), p. 7.

Session 6: Telling It Like It Is
1. Adapted from Jim Burns, *Uncommon Youth Ministry* (Ventura, CA: Gospel Light, 2008), p. 26.

Session 7: Listening to God
1. In this parable about the different types of soil, Jesus used imagery that would have been familiar to all of His listeners. In Palestine, there were two ways to sow seed, and both ways—tossing it on the ground or tying a sack of seeds on the back of a donkey—caused some seeds to land in places where they wouldn't grow. Farmers usually made their fields in long narrow strips, leaving room between each strip for walking. As the farmers walked, this ground

became packed as hard as pavement. This is the ground that Jesus calls "the wayside." It was also common for the soil in Palestine to have a layer of stone underneath. When Jesus refers to the stony ground, He is probably referring to this type of soil over stone.

Session 8: Faith

1. Jesus' use of the analogy of "faith moving mountains" was nothing new to His listeners. Jesus takes this idea directly from the way people viewed skilled teachers of the day. A great teacher who could really expound and interpret Scripture was known as an uprooter or a pulverizer of mountains. To tear up, uproot or even pulverize were all regular phrases for removing difficulties. The essence of what Jesus is saying is, "If you have enough faith, even the hardest task can be accomplished." See William Barclay, *The Gospel of Matthew*, vol. 2 (Philadelphia, PA: The Westminster Press, 1958), pp. 184-185.

Session 9: Gifted by God

1. A talent weighed about 75 pounds. The value of a talent depended on the kind of metal being weighed—copper, silver or gold—and it came to be used as a unit of coinage backed by the precious metal. In this passage in Matthew, although the talent clearly represents a large sum of money, there is nothing to show the exact value intended. (A similar parable with slightly different details involving the *mina* appears in Luke 19:12-27.)
2. Adapted from Lawrence C. and Andrea J. Enscoe, "The Right Equipment" *Skit'omatic* (Ventura, CA: Gospel Light, 1993), pp. 74-75.

Session 10: Living Our Faith

1. Jesus' use of salt in this passage would have made sense to His listeners because salt was highly valued in Jesus' day. The Greeks called salt "divine." The Romans believed that salt was the purest of all things, because it came from the purest all places—the sun and the sea. At the end of the day, Jewish sacrifices were offered with salt. Salt was also a preservative. In Jesus' day, it was used to keep food from going bad and was even used to keep decay from getting worse. And salt was also used for healing—in the Old Testament, newborn babies were bathed and salted (see Ezekiel 16:4). See William Barclay, *The Gospel of Matthew*, vol. I (Philadelphia, PA: The Westminster Press, 1958), pp. 114-116.

Session 11: Forgiveness

1. Jesus reached back into history in this parable. Based on passages in the Old Testament such as Amos 1:3-13 and 2:1-6, the Jews had deduced that God's forgiveness extended three times, and then, on the fourth offense, His punishment was released. Man was not thought to be more gracious than God, so it was believed that man could only forgive three times. See William Barclay, *The Gospel of Matthew*, vol. 2 (Philadelphia, PA: The Westminster Press, 1958), pp. 212-213.

More *Uncommon* Resources for Leaders

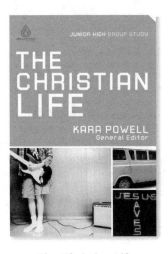

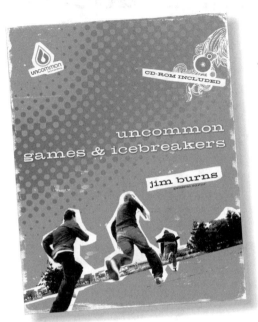
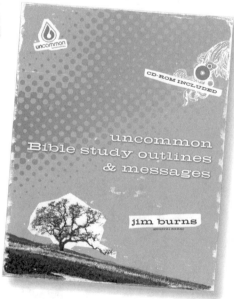